bad fire

A Memoir of Disruption

Tucker Lieberman

copylight

Copyright © 2024 Glyph Torrent (Bogotá, Colombia)

Cover design by Tucker Lieberman. All interior art also by Tucker Lieberman, unless it is obviously by someone else.

Fonts: The cover has the title in lowercase **plakat=fraktur** and the author name in IMPACT LABEL. The text is Goudy Old Style with chapter headings and drop-caps in lowercase humboldtfraktur, and the book title and author name appear in the page headers in IMPACT LABEL.

Author photo courtesy Alexandria Mauck Photography www.alexandriamauck.com

This is a work of nonfiction. Why would I make this up. I would have made up something else.

All rights reserved. Don't steal bad fire. Really bad idea.

First paperback edition: December 30, 2018

Second paperback edition: January 1, 2021

Third paperback edition: November 12, 2024

ISBN-13: 978-1-7329060-3-7

bad fire

intro/duct/chim[ney]	1
bad fire	15
a:drought the author	185
sight:ashes	187

Engraving by Gerard Jollain. "The Death of Nadab and Abihu." From La Saincte Bible: Contenant le Vieil et le Nouveau Testament (Enrichie de plusieurs belles figures), *1670.*

intro/duct/chim[ney]

Disaster doesn't look like yelling and waving. In a crisis, we never feel exactly whatever we anticipated we'd feel, either.

Bad Fire is a memoir of anxiety, suicidal hallucination, acid reflux, unintentional weight loss, and medication. Though the topics may be stressful, I hope there's benefit in exploring them. I extend to those readers this gentle warning and invitation.

I interpret the Biblical story of Nadav and Avihu from a Jewish-and-atheist perspective, reaching an unorthodox conclusion.

I discuss capitalist perspectives on how people show up at the office.

Taking the caterpillar-to-butterfly metaphor for life change, especially as it is often applied to gender transition, this narrative lets that insect go a little wild.

This is a story about how a small collapse looks from the outside and how it feels on the inside.

Mostly, it's about letting go and letting become.

In *Bad Fire*, you may read my partial rejection of the term "illness" as it applies to a specific situation I experienced. What other words can I use? Perhaps I suffered from "too muchness," as Rachel Vorona Cote names the emotionality and self-determination with which women defy prudish and hierarchical constraints.[1] The social judgment implied in the "too much" is what may make us feel or seem ill. You, reader, can decide.

This is my "limit text," to use Lance Olsen's phrase: an example of using a "disturbance" to test the limits of storytelling so that we, together, "can never quite think of it in the same way again."[2] What is the "it": the disturbance or the storytelling? Both, I hope.

As a bonus: *Reading this book will make you trans.* You have come to the right place. Even if you do not want to be made trans, you are in the right place. The right place may not be about what you want.

On Illness

In *The Wounded Storyteller*, Arthur Frank says that, when overwhelming illness strikes, we live immersed in "chaos stories" that aren't yet proper stories. Pain obliterates us. We hardly even have a self. We are, as he uses Elaine Scarry's phrase, "unmaking the world." Only much later "the voice of chaos can be identified and a story reconstructed." The narrative we make of an illness will depend on our social context and is related to three other kinds of story we can tell about ourselves: "spiritual autobiographies, stories of becoming a man or a woman and what that gender identity involves, and finally survivor stories of inflicted traumas." We tell these stories to map ourselves back into the world and relearn how to navigate on a new journey. Ideally, the illness narrative connects us and asks if we are caring for ourselves and others. The audience must do a special kind of listening too, Frank says. What we say *about* our bodies comes *through* our bodies.[3]

On Running at Night

This is a memoir about running at night. It's my perspective as a white trans man.

I ran around Boston at night because I was mentally ill, and I felt safe doing so. Being on the street at night gave more rein to my mental illness and may have magnified it. I floridly exercised my demons and indulged the fantasy that I was fighting them. My running at night arguably wasn't motivated by real concerns and was minimally grounded in reality. The physical activity through which I tried to stanch emotional pain may also have entertained and prolonged that pain.

White supremacy wants people of all races to believe that whiteness — that is, the construct of whiteness, and anything that flows from it — is the best way to be. One way that racism shows up is in the assumption that someone's mental illness is "better" (less threatening, more manageable, more rule-abiding, more artistically generative, or morally superior) just because the person is white. This is an assumption we can actively drop. People have different experiences, and we can observe differences without jumping to the judgment of "better" or "worse."

If whiteness influences a white person's mental illness, then whiteness is hurting the white person too, all the more so if they don't spot what's happening or are in denial about it.

If we aren't grounded in ourselves, it's tough to begin the work. But once we see the dynamics in ourselves and those around us, we'll know more about what we must learn and do.

In Judaism, the repair of the world is called *tikkun olam*. The work does not end. If we do the work today, we can hope for results in our lifetimes. We can strive for better collective outcomes.

The crisis we avert may be our own.

This book explores natural unfoldings. Change can happen on its own; wait, don't push. Of course, sometimes it's better to push. Weigh that idea in the balance.

You already have all the permission you need, but I give you my permission, too, if you're waiting on it to flex your wings.

The Binary Is Calling From Outside the House

A remark on my gender to orient you to this memoir.

Remember that *this book will make you trans*, and please permit the magic to work.

Born female and given a girl's name, I didn't think much about gender until I reached adolescence, when I picked a more masculine-sounding name and asked people to call me "he." Around my eighteenth birthday, I began testosterone, surgically reshaped my chest, and legally changed my name and gender markers on all my IDs. In this way, I'm a trans man, or what I thought of back then as a transsexual man. I use language I'm comfortable with to describe myself. Other people use different language for themselves.

(If readers don't already have a basic idea of what a trans man is, I hope just now I've given enough context.)

I didn't want to be "trans" *per se*. I would have asked to have been reborn as a cis man. My transness arose as a desire for a brief journey toward a masculine destination. Yet that has made my transness a permanent feature of my life. It's a fact about me.

Today I'm forty-four, living contentedly with the results of the changes I made when I was a teenager.

My gender is *dayenu*, "enough." It doesn't need to be examined under a microscope or fussed over. It doesn't need to be lamented or denied. It is sufficient for my life. I am allowed to live as a man.

There are other ways, as a human being, I'm required to change.

My gender is boring, but not so boring that the world hands me obvious words for it.

I find myself fitting a lot of the slots that are recognizably "men's," as I originally intended when I transitioned. I picked a major battle against the category of "woman" being applied to me. Emotionally I haven't chafed against the category of "man," nor do I worry anymore about exactly how I count or fit in as one, even when that label isn't a perfect fit. On a personal level, I'm no longer distressed by my sex and gender; the home I've made is my home.

Like everyone else, I was born into a world with gender norms, and I deal with them. I let them absorb me, or I resist them gently. Each of us conforms or resists with varying levels of consciousness and intention. Like many, I've found my own equilibrium, and the ways I gender myself and allow myself to be gendered are predictable.

But we who are alive are always on the move.

On the Trans Memoir

What makes a memoir trans, you might ask, *apart from its authorship by someone who happens to be trans?*

You are going to know the answer by the end of this book. Sit by the cocoon and watch what emerges. It will make itself obvious. You may not have words to explain it, but you'll know it when you see it. It will appear in a cascade of words, and the answer will be an artifact of those words, as light implies shadow, as shadow implies light, an interplay of binary meanings.

Since that's a tease, I'll give an alternate answer, but this next answer, too, will be indirect.

Many trans people feel prompted to clarify whether we are *nonbinary trans* or, to use a backformation, *binary trans*.

As I've said, I'm relatively comfortable functioning as a man — that is, as what the gender binary considers a man. Additionally, the word *trans* (or, antiquely, "transsexual") is accurate and feels adequate.

Nonbinary and *binary* aren't labels I apply to myself. Here are reasons.

My sense is that many who use the word *nonbinary* do so to distinguish their gender flavor from mine. I'm overjoyed that not everyone is me, and I support them expressing who they are with their own words. I have no plans to steal their gender label and water down its nonbinary power with my transsexuality. Their label will work best for them when I get out of its way.

Nonetheless, not calling myself *nonbinary* doesn't make me *binary*. Yes, I function within my society's man-woman gender binary. But I'm not binary in my essence. I don't believe in a soul, and the soul I don't have isn't binary. I had a sex change, for crying out loud. I am a sacred androgyne. If I have kvetched about what I am or refused the call to my fated androgynous role at some given moment, that makes my life a Campbellian hero's journey, but it doesn't mean I'm a black-and-white thinker. I simultaneously inhabit-and-resist the gender binary. I don't control this; I wake up in the morning this way. I'm binary-and-nonbinary when I let my beard grow just as much as when I shave it. I can't crawl in nor out of this box-and-nonbox I (haven't) put myself in. Choosing between the labels *nonbinary* and *binary* would obscure my experience. So I refuse to choose, and I don't call myself by either word.

By the way, sometimes people say *binary trans*, but no one ever says *binary cis*. If cis people don't have to know whether they're binary or nonbinary, neither should trans people have to choose this label. Humans do not reduce to two types: those who have to assert whether we're *binary* or *nonbinary* and those who are off the hook. We each accept-and-challenge the man/woman binary in our own unique way.

If the binary in question is the cis/trans binary, well, I engage-and-challenge that one too. I don't need a gender label if its only purpose is to make cis people comfortable, enable them to extract information about my trans life or let them classify me. By refusing to answer the question of "Are you binary or nonbinary?" on cis-dominant terms, I'm breaking down the cis/trans binary a little bit, even as I position myself as trans to do so.

Lastly, I recognize that not everyone is inside "the binary." Though I've switched my position between the two dominant gender teams, that doesn't imply that I view the world only in terms of those two teams.

Obviously, there are other possibilities. Nonbinary people are nonbinary. I recognize that the two dominant genders do not constitute an inescapable binary. That means there is no binary with which I can identify myself. There are two majority genders, yes, but it'd be self-contradictory for me to identify as *binary* while bucking even the tiniest gender stereotype.

That's five reasons. I'm fond of five-reason lists. As I wrote in my book *Ten Past Noon*: "*Because because because because because* is a song lyric from Oz honoring manifest wizardry."

Having spoken in that artery, I continue in this vein:

You can call yourself *binary* if you like, but you do not become an *exemplum* of a binary just because one side pleases you more than the other. You exist in ways that are comprehensible to the system and in ways that are not. The system's engagement of your attention doesn't make you an example of the system.

The Little Mermaid wanted to leave the sea and become human. She couldn't be amphibious, but she was granted a transitional period of human-becoming during which she knew that, once she succeeded in her quest, the change would be permanent and she could never return to the sea. Her choice was binary. She accepted that condition and made her choice within the binary parameters. Her identity, however, isn't clearly binary. A mermaid is part fish and part human to begin with, and that's what makes her a mermaid, which is a third thing. When she leaves behind her fish qualities to become fully human, in some sense we think of her as still "really" a mermaid. She has lungs and legs now, but she'll always be part mermaid on the inside. Come to think, why say "part"? Say "full." She can be fully human and simultaneously fully mermaid. A human can have an imaginary fish in her, and we can honor her memory of the sea.

We may "happen to" conform to binaries, or at least we may appear to. Surviving within a binary system does not imply that we fully embrace it; we may adapt to it without consciously identifying with it, explicitly endorsing it, or otherwise exemplifying it.

A binary may eventually dissolve on its own. And we'll adapt to the new situation.

We can "live with binaries" (alongside or within them) without "being binary." Or, for those who prefer this language: We can "be binary" through our existential and pragmatic doings without establishing any permanent, objective binary truth about what we "really" are.

My goal for this book is a trans goal. I want all readers to feel a distinctly trans feeling. It's a recruitment, an invitation. It may be most effective when it is a surprise.

Here we'll cup a butterfly in the hand, feeling it pulse its wings open and shut. A butterfly has two left wings and two right wings, and that equipment is useful for flight, but the butterfly isn't binary. It's a living being. It didn't grow from a not-butterfly; it grew from a *caterpillar*, which both is and isn't a butterfly. Caterpillars and butterflies aren't opposites. A caterpillar butterflies itself in a way that is gorgeously unexpected.

Craft History of *Bad Fire*

Bad Fire centers on a mental disruption I experienced in 2015 when I was 35. I could not write about the chaos while I was still in it. This is a challenge for life and art: to let life and art take time.

Over a couple weeks in 2018, I wrote a brief memoir. Sharon Annable, Arturo Serrano, and Brontë Wieland provided helpful suggestions on early drafts, and Alexandria Mauck photographed me at a firewalking event.

That first version of *Bad Fire* was self-published for New Year's 2019 through only one distributor. As many as two dozen paperback copies were produced, most of which I bought and mailed to individuals and organizations who I thought might want them. Sam Hearne interviewed me for the Men's Health Arkive (an audio recording was made), and Maribel Garcia interviewed me for Book Club Babble (the text is online).

After publication, I spent another two years tinkering with the text, using the existing narrative as scaffolding. Félix González Montejo helped me identify points for clarification. Riana Good passed along a paper by Rabbi Ora Weiss that mentioned Moses' investigation [*darosh darash*] into a matter about a goat. I had further insights into the story of Nadav and Avihu which I published on the JewishBoston blog and in *Shalom Magazine*,[4] and I put a few key lines from those essays into the second version of *Bad Fire*. I originally shared the song playlist in my guest blog post for Anne Davis ("Crisis: A Playlist," *Running in Shadows*, May 27, 2020).

I added ideas that would not let me go. I traded horsepower and brevity for depth and completeness. I provided more analysis and levity to cushion the emotional intensity. It takes longer to wiggle in and out of the story. I quote a number of other writers because, although this is still "my story," it has evolved into a set of public-facing ideas I can weigh against other ideas in literature. It is as much philosophy as memoir. It is atheist Bible interpretation. It will make you trans.

Rabbi Levi Alter and Venus Davis provided feedback in late 2020. Jenson Books in Logan, Utah helped me locate a copy of Peter Chadwick's essay after I had unwisely relinquished my own copy of that hard-to-find paperback. My mother, Linda Lieberman, dug out some of my baby photos. The second version of *Bad Fire* was self-published for New Year's 2021.

Then I came up with more ideas, and that's why you're holding the third version of *Bad Fire*, published in late 2024.

I've reused the same ISBN for all three versions. This is a librarian sin, but no copies of my earlier versions ever made it to a library, so no librarians are mad at me. The 13-digit ISBN bumps along like a caterpillar, and this book, too, wants to keep its original DNA as it becomes a butterfly.

You're unlikely to find earlier versions, as it was print-on-demand and you can no longer demand that an earlier copy be printed. An original copy is a collector's item, worth a billion dollars. But the version you hold in your hands right now is worth even more. *Because it will make you trans.*

This Is About You Too

I'm telling what I've witnessed, and I invite you to witness my telling.

My suffering wasn't exceptional, regardless of how it felt to me at the time; I just had my own process of interpreting it. I share my story as an example of an interpretive process. Please renew your own permission to be kind to yourself when you do something similar. May my words reveal some empathetic insight — known in the body as music, released into flight again, now with lyrics — that you can apply someday when caring for yourself or others.

Our attention will always direct itself a bit off-course, which may just be the unfolding of a surprise. Our attention won't optimize. Let's not worry about it.

Any story displaces the attention that the listener might have given to another story. If we're excessively nervous about our finite time on Earth and we spend our days ranking the relative importance of stories, we will never listen to any stories at all.

The Worst Possible Life Disaster (for me or for someone else) wouldn't necessarily yield up the Best Possible Story (for you). The best possible story is different for each audience member. It depends what you want. I offer this story from a place of humility, and I trust in your judgment to spend your time as you wish. If you are bored, close the book. But then the story will not make you trans.

While I don't need very many people to read this book (the social labor alone would be tiring for me), I'd like for people who need it to find it. I'd be grateful if you would help others who would love *Bad Fire* to meet up with it.

I appreciate everyone who supported me or put up with me during my "research" for this book. I mean, of course, when I was having a bad year or two.

I appreciate all my readers for your time.

May something in here speak to you. May you be trans. May you be fire.

bad fire

Wolf with butterfly wings starting the race.

When I was thirteen, anticipating the assignment of a Torah portion for my Bat Mitzvah, I hoped the portion would contain a message personally tailored for me about the mysteries of the cosmos.

Consider how Moses stops to look at the burning bush. That was the kind of story I wanted. Moses, born to an enslaved Jewish woman, is adopted in infancy by an Egyptian princess and has a comfortable life in the palace. As a young man, he begins to wrestle with his ethnic roots and his proper role in the world. He takes a moral side, irrevocably so, by killing one of the royal oppressors. Now his own life is forfeit. No one can help him, as his true tribe remains enslaved. Under stress, he runs away.

In the desert, he sees fire that isn't really fire; it doesn't destroy what it seems to burn. That's God getting his attention. The fire signals the One of the Unpronounceable Name, YHVH. Moses wants a closer look, but God warns him off. Moses covers his face as if he recognizes that his own subjectivity is a key to unlock this experience.

God tells Moses to confront the king and demand the liberation of his people. "But," Moses asks, "who shall I say sent me?" *"Ehyeh asher ehyeh,"* replies God. "I will be who I will be. Tell them 'I Will Be' sent you."

Moses, raised as royalty, had assumed his life was preordained and self-contained. Then he punctured his own bubble. He made breathing room to let in new experiences.

In Hebrew, vowels were not always written. Who would think or dare, as David Abram asked in *The Spell of the Sensuous*, to visually represent "sounded breath"? Yet it's useful to indicate vowels, so writers often leveraged certain consonants to represent them. If the consonants in God's name, YHVH, were meant to be pronounced as vowels, then the name of God is a breath. The name might sound something like *ehyeh asher ehyeh*: becoming. The name, Abram says, "may not be separable from the mystery of breathing — this ebb and flow that ceaselessly binds us to the invisible."[5]

The burning bush would have been an exciting Torah portion to discuss for my Bat Mitzvah.

To my disappointment, my portion was *Shemini*, covering Chapters 9–11 of Leviticus. (This assignment was foreseeable, as the portions are assigned to children based on their own birthdays.)

In *Shemini*, Moses, having long since seen the burning bush and having led the Hebrews to freedom across the Red Sea, wanders through the desert, taking instructions from God. He summons Aaron and instructs him to bring ruminants — goats, cows, sheep — to sacrifice to God, in return for which God is supposed to reveal Himself. Aaron does exactly as he's told in gruesome detail. He fingerpaints the altar with animal blood. He dismembers the animals from head to toe, shakes their body parts in a "wave offering," and burns them — including kidney, liver, and fat — on the altar as "sin offerings," "burnt offerings," and "peace offerings." All of this is acceptable, ritually and otherwise, according to the narrator's implicit assessment.

Reading this passage today, I mentally insert KC Green's famous *Gunshow* webcomic panel of a dog sitting at the kitchen table with a cup of coffee, saying, as the house burns down and just before the dog's own face melts off, "This is fine."[6] My sarcasm comes from my prejudice that, really, fingerpainting with blood does not seem fine to me, and I am skeptical about normalizing it. Any personal message meant for me in this Torah portion was a bad omen.

Leaving aside our modern rejection of animal sacrifice, the bigger problem within the text is that two of Aaron's sons, Nadav and Avihu, improvise part of the ritual. They make an unauthorized sacrificial fire. God immediately responds with bigger fire, consuming them. Moses says to Aaron, "I told you so. This is God's holiness and glory. Dump their bodies outside the camp and don't mourn them." There is no resurrection; they are dead. We never hear about them again. We know nothing about them except their names. As if they were too queer, too sick, too *avant garde*, too violent. We are never told exactly what was wrong with the way they presented their sacrifice.

This is a change from God's admonishment to Cain in Genesis 4. There, God tells Cain his sacrifice can't be accepted until Cain becomes a good person, suggesting that God values a sacrifice based on the supplicant's character. By *Shemini*, though, it seems God's patience has worn through. Now, there's no more sincerely offered life guidance, just pettiness. Without judging the character of Aaron's sons, and ensuring that all that will be remembered of them is their ritual inaccuracy, God incinerates them. Ritual remains God's recurring concern. God will later warn in no uncertain terms that more of Aaron's sons will die if they don't use a special handwashing station before they enter the ritual space (Exodus 30:17–21). Aaron does not have infinite sons.

Everyone at the scene of Nadav and Avihu's death is instructed not to talk about what they've witnessed, a social mistake I now recognize as a sure-fire recipe for emotional trauma.

It seems the text's message to readers today is that there are some things we're not supposed to question.

It happened, and it was God. The more we overthink it, the madder God gets.

A popular interpretation is that Nadav and Avihu were drunk when they offered bad fire. This is because they were mentioned earlier at a feast ("they had a vision of the Divine, and they ate and drank," Exodus 24:11) and because, after God burns them to death, God immediately declares that it will be a capital crime for Aaron and his remaining sons to drink intoxicants in the holy space (Leviticus 10:8-9). The commentary of Rashi, an 11th-century French rabbi, affirms the possibility that they were drunk.[7]

But this interpretation implies that Nadav and Avihu deserved to die for having a beer. God may feel that way, but no one else does.

At thirteen, I had to prepare a brief talk to the congregation about what this passage meant. A year or two away from figuring out my own queerness, I was already enough of a nonconformist that lighting a fire the wrong way didn't seem like a big deal. Another disappointment with this passage: Its name, *Shemini* (Hebrew for "eighth," as in, "On the eighth day..."), turned out not to rhyme with "apple pie" (which would have sounded totally mystical, like the zodiac sign Gemini) but rather with "bikini" (a garment I intended never to wear).

Still, I had to work with what I was given. I insisted on printing the line "For today the Lord will appear to you" (Leviticus 9:4) on my Bat Mitzvah invitations. In its proper context, this phrase was Moses' justification for why a half-dozen animals had to be sacrificed. It was the prelude to the unplanned conflagration of Aaron's sons. I was hoping to bend its meaning to herald a more gentle, transformative divine revelation that somehow had to do with me.

A reasonable reading is that Nadav and Avihu's offense was an accident. If so, the best moral takeaway is that they didn't deserve to be punished so severely, but this is probably not what one is supposed to say in synagogue.

We may be expected to say something like: If we do ever receive instructions from God, we should follow them to the letter. Furthermore, we should follow local custom, lest God be displeased that we care so little about our own community's culture. Finally, we should watch our backs in case God kicks us for no reason.

For my Bat Mitzvah, after some rumination, I gave a speech saying *God is upset when you do a half-assed job.* Sounds true.

I might also have cautioned about the risk of religious innovation. That message didn't feel genuine to me. Religious innovation can't really hurt us. I always knew this. Innovation ties into themes of gender, sexuality, art, growing into our own power, challenging people who claim to have exclusive truth, and being honest with ourselves so that we can open to real connection with others. The Indigo Girls' song "Strange Fire," which I would hear later in high school, is about just this.

The story's a reverse Prometheus. Prometheus stole good fire from the gods, for which the gods sentenced him to be pecked at by an eagle for eternity, immortal and suffering. Aaron's sons offered bad fire to the One God, and the One God obliterated them on the spot before they knew what had happened. Both stories are framed as warnings about innovation and arrogance, yet at the same time, the stories seem designed for the listener to sympathize with Prometheus and with Aaron's sons, as they didn't do anything wrong.

Really, Prometheus did nothing wrong. Fire isn't a thing, it's a process. Bring your own firewood and touch it to someone else's fire to light it up. You're not depriving anyone else of their fire. How can you steal fire if it's not a thing?

We are always up against forces that want to reconstruct the past. There are Jews who are worried that we have forgotten the exact species of snail called *khilazon* so we can't smash it to make the blue dye called *tekhelet* and can't wear the properly colored sacred fringe at our hips, which leads them to conclude that, rather than innovate the dye, we should just wait for the Messiah to come and give us the snail so we're absolutely sure we've got the true indigo. This is an avoidance of innovation made very literal.

I was never afraid of innovation, but I couldn't conjure any other interpretation of the Nadav and Avihu story.

If I'd been older, I might have suggested the more atheistic reading that Aaron's sons were smeared with animal fat, weren't careful with their fire sacrifice, and set their own tunics ablaze, and that their community rationalized the terrible accident by saying the boys had incurred God's wrath. Bad fire.

At thirteen, though, I settled for giving an inadequate sermon. I assumed this passage bore no correspondence to the way the world actually worked or to anything that was going to happen in my life. More present to my mind was my annoyance that I had to wear a dress to my Bat Mitzvah and my nervousness that I would trip in my high heels and drop the Torah.

"most people know what it is like to be seriously afraid," Elyn Saks begins. She contrasts ordinary fear with her typical feeling of "disorganization" during schizophrenic episodes, the latter being "much harder, and weirder, to describe."

> Consciousness gradually loses its coherence. One's center gives way. The center cannot hold. The "me" becomes a haze, and the solid center from which one experiences reality breaks up like a bad radio signal. There is no longer a sturdy vantage point from which to look out, take things in, assess what's happening. No core holds things together, providing the lens through which to see the world, to make judgments and comprehend risk. Random moments of time follow one

> another. No organizing principle takes successive moments in time and puts them together in a coherent way from which sense can be made. And it's all taking place in slow motion.[8]

I have not experienced schizophrenia. That's a brain disease I don't have. Nevertheless, these particular words of Saks's do mean something for me insofar as, for an extended period, my life lost some coherence, both embodied and conceptual. I don't have a label for whatever it is that I did experience. The words quoted above might speak to people in different ways, are probably better than similar words I could invent, and might apply to a variety of other mental experiences. Grief, for one.

Speaking of grief, Matthew Salesses asks: What falls apart, and at what do we believe we are succeeding when we say we are "holding it together"? He proposes that "one's life is not the *it* coming apart. The *it* is one's sense of reality," also known as "what makes one real to oneself."[9]

Whether one holds it together determines whether the play becomes comedy or tragedy. Lauren Berlant draws this distinction:

> In the situation comedy, the subject whose world is not too destabilized by a 'situation' that arises performs a slapstick maladjustment that turns out absurdly and laughably, without destroying very much. In the situation tragedy, the subject's world is fragile beyond repair, one gesture away from

losing all access to sustaining its fantasies: the situation threatens utter, abject unraveling.[10]

eir ibn Gabbai's kabbalistic book *Tola'at Ya'akov*, written in 1507, used the image of a worm [tola'at] to represent the Jews, his people. Worms are oral, and (so he says) the Jews are too, as we recite prayer, scripture, law. We destroy and socially reconstruct using words. One kind of tola'at worm may chew down a cedar tree (representing the enemy). Another, the silkworm, chews to make silk, a beautiful gift to God.[11]

Unfortunately for the worm, others boil it to harvest the silk. I feel that's relevant too.

wo days after my Bat Mitzvah ceremony, I recorded a dream: "You walk in the rain to school. You hold two memory disks. One has problems and profound insight into them. The other has quick solutions."

s a teenager, I was the youngest member in an adult poetry workshop group at the library. One day when I did not have a poem of my own to share, I brought "Change" by Ellen Bass. "This is the moment when the ancient fears / race like thoroughbreds, asking for more / and more rein," she writes. It's a poem for people in a more advanced stage of life than I had yet attained. "I am hoisting a car from mud ruts / half a century deep."¹² The grownups liked it very much.

I also had a bilingual anthology of Latin American poetry. When Juana de Ibarbourou was in her late twenties, she wrote "Mujer" ("Woman"), which opens:

> Si yo fuera hombre, ¡qué hartazgo de luna,
> de sombra y silencio me había de dar!
> ¡Cómo, noche a noche, solo ambularía
> por los campos quietos y por frente al mar!

> If I were a man, I'd get to have my fill of it:
> such a fill of moon, shadow, and silence!
> How I'd walk alone, night after night
> through the still fields and along the beach!¹³

At the time, I thought "hartazgo de luna," the bellyfullness of taking in as much moonlight as you can stomach, was a pretty line. I lived in a suburb where there were many large fields and the houses were spaced far apart. Now I understand that many women are afraid to walk at night at all, and it would be a liberation from fear to enjoy an abundance of moonlight. There may be a reference here to the moon's monthly cycle; perhaps the poet has had enough of *that* and is proposing that it stop cycling already. It would, if she were a man.

Through my school, I entered a haiku in a national contest. I miscounted the syllables, but it won an award anyway. I specified that there were nine dewdrops on a spiderweb, not because I was educated in any haiku tradition in which this number had secret meaning but because that is the sort of detail I would log. Rita Dove, then the U.S. Poet Laureate, wrote me a letter of congratulations.

Dove has a poem titled "History" that begins:

> Everything's a metaphor, some wise
> guy said, and his woman nodded, wisely.
> Why was this such a discovery
> to him? Why did history
> happen only on the outside?
> She'd watched an embryo track an arc
> across her swollen belly from the inside...[14]

This poem was already part of the world then (though I did not yet know it) and is part of history now. I like what Dove offers here as a definition of metaphor: that which is not yet concrete because it is internal, that which is part of you though it has a life of its own.

My ordinary tween-age desire for psychic superpowers waned in favor of the idea that I could change my sex, a more scientifically attainable project.

At fifteen, I picked a new name for myself. Tucker seemed about right. Later, when I made it legal, I added a middle name, Brent, whose sound I also liked.

I didn't choose these names for their etymology, though I was aware of what they meant. "Tucker" referred to the meat-tenderizing approach to softening leather or cloth, and so it came to mean a tailor; farther back in Old English it had meant one who "tortures" or "torments." "Brent" also had Old English and Germanic roots meaning simply "burned," as, for example, a criminal might have been branded as punishment. The two names together signify the one who afflicts and the one who is afflicted. If I had picked the rough Hebrew equivalent, it might have been *Ud*, as in what God said of the high priest Joshua: "Isn't this one a firebrand snatched from the flames?"[15]

I supposed, if the meanings of my name would be relevant to my life story, I'd find out when it happened.

When I was eighteen, I filled a large notebook with what I called a "spiritual journal." I sought a virtuous purity indistinguishable from inner peace. I had no definition of it. I assumed I could achieve virtue and peace by overthinking and transcribing every passing thought over a period of six weeks.

It is OK to laugh at a spiritual journal if it is your own. In a bloated style, I wrote a series of platitudes and unacknowledged contradictions. The journal's original aim, "discovering my purpose," was undercut by my own admission that I did not believe such truths existed to be found. I had no methodology for discovering my life's purpose and failed to make the tiniest inroad toward it.

Soon I went away to college where my attention was redirected for the usual reasons. I abandoned the journal with no conclusion.

The odd thing was that I wasted pages at a moment when I had something worth writing about. I'd been taking a high dose of testosterone for six months and, only one month before starting to write, I'd had surgery to reshape my chest as part of my transition from female to male.

I refused to write about this.

I don't remember why. I probably didn't yet know how to talk about being transgender from a perspective of long-awaited fulfillment rather than frustration. Since I was simultaneously going off to college, I probably sought new pursuits: anything but gender. (Vaguely, I wanted to become a scientist to save the rainforest.) I was priming the pump by testing my ability to churn out new sentences. *Certainly* – I can imagine my eighteen-year-old self saying – *I know what is relevant to my spiritual life and what is not, thank you very much!*

Thus I made overreaching, foolish interpretations in this journal.

When someone I'd known since I was a young girl asked me at Shabbat services if I was "new to the congregation," I felt peaceful and happy. I was happy to have passed as a man. Someone who had attached me to a female template now found me unrecognizable. Good. In the journal, however, I attributed my sensation of inner peace to the cultivation of my own spiritual virtues (ahem).

In another entry, I announced I no longer needed gay community, since it was "facile," operated with "rudimentary definitions," and presented me with "no intellectual challenge." Well. As an eighteen-year-old gay-identified kid who had barely been around any other gay people, I was rather obviously trying to hide a deep-seated fear that gay men would never accept me. I had plenty to learn from gay men and wanted to do so. My real problem was that the parameters of that community seemed to exclude me and I didn't know what to do about it. I lacked the ideological, political, and social prowess needed to deal with my exclusion, so I journaled privately to give myself the illusion of intellectual and spiritual control. My attitude was: *I don't need gay community. I am too evolved.*

I only noticed these flaws when, twenty years later, I found and reread my "spiritual journal," wincing a little. My younger self hadn't been honest and clear even in my private writings. I'd planned to obfuscate until I rose to a rarefied plane. That's the recipe for neither good introspection nor good writing. The pages amounted to handwriting practice.

We may build the infrastructure for thoughts and feelings before we have any substance to fill that vessel. All hat and no cattle. Hundreds of pages about what we'd do with an idea if we caught one. Some teenagers pop off the shelf as good communicators, but I was not one of them.

Having unpacked the old journal, I made a final decision. The journal was not historically valuable. Even if I become historically significant someday, no librarian should ever have to curate that notebook in any manuscript collection and no well-meaning grad student should ever have to stumble across it. The journal had to die. I uncurated it. I murdered all one hundred and twenty pages with scissors and a recycle bin.

The inadequacy of the scribbles in that eighteen-year-old's journal are best described in light of the dream I'd recorded when I was thirteen. *"You hold two memory disks. One has problems and profound insight into them. The other has quick solutions."* In the dream, why didn't I just keep the solution disk and throw out the problem disk? If I knew the answers to my internal conflict, why was I still obsessing? Maybe I didn't believe the answers I held in my hand.

The subjects I wrote about then were not the subjects I needed to write about. Good intentions that don't correspond to the needs of the moment may as well be sins.

"Glass beads shatter on / spider's tiny florid handiwork / nine tears of the night." That was my contest-winning haiku in eighth grade. Haikus have a 5-7-5 syllable count, but my middle line has 9 syllables. That was my error. Yet at last my contest award makes sense to me. The dewdrop-and-spiderweb mess is brilliantly described as "nine tears" because the nine-syllable line breaks the mold and wrecks the haiku. I wrote a haiku that gained consciousness and became renegade free verse.

I swear this was an accident. I remember committing no such intentional wit. But the poem tells on itself. It calls itself out. The grownups must have thought I did it on purpose.

This is the sort of artistic mistake that Boston Philharmonic conductor Benjamin Zander told students to honor by exclaiming: "How fascinating!"[16]

Looking back, it's clear: This haiku made me trans.

> Nine tears: a haiku?
> Weeping spider bit me. "You shall be
> trans within the year."

though I was spiritually curious in my teens and early twenties, I eventually accepted that I'm an atheist. I'm not mad at religion, and I don't want to be rude to religious people. After all, no God exists to be impressed by my bravado in what I say about his nonexistence. I just don't think there's a God, that's all.

I want to write what I believe. Honesty usually improves a message.

my left hip was deformed from birth. We don't know exactly why this happens, but it may be that the fetus is squeezed too tightly in the womb.

Think about how ambivalent the fetus must feel about this. It needs to stretch its legs, but it also needs to stay exactly where it is for a long time because if it leaves the womb too early it won't be able to breathe.

As an infant, I was placed in an orthopedic harness until it was time for me to walk.

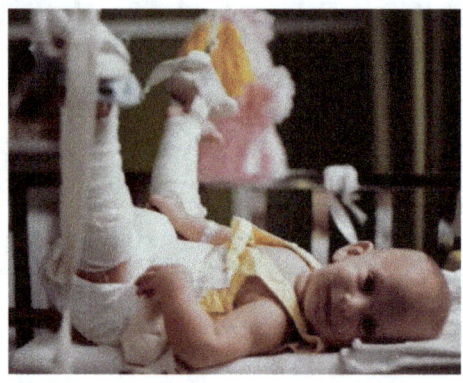

In traction at the hospital

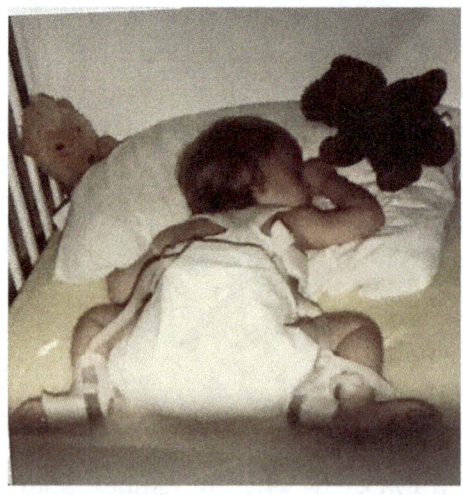

Sleeping in the harness

Just sitting

I walk normally as an adult, but the feeling of walking with this hip is the feeling of pushing a grocery cart with one wheel that keeps spinning and skewing outward in the wrong direction. I have to nudge it to go forward, forward, forward, and it's viable as long as I don't put too much food in the cart.

In college, I asked my doctor why I could no longer eat as many brownies as I liked without gaining weight. The doctor answered: "You turned twenty." This metabolic revelation did not persuade me to stop eating brownies. The Meeting Street Cafe used what must have been an entire stick of butter to make a single chocolate chip cookie as big as my face. There was a sandwich shop called Geoff's where friends who ate meat ordered the bacon-laced Kevorkian or its kosher-style sibling, the Rachel, while I ordered the vegetarian Monster Lisa or the Dead Head.

I put too much food in the cart.

When I reached my mid-thirties, something complicated happened to me. I cannot and will not explain all the backstory here. It was a turning point in the long-running TV series of my life. If you'd like a fictionalized version, read my 2022 novel, *Most Famous Short Film of All Time*.

Let's just set the scene:

I was single, no kids, no pets. I had a good job that I liked and cared about, and only a few months earlier I had bought myself a condo on the edge of Boston, just where the city officially becomes the suburbs, with a mortgage for which I was solely responsible.

I was overly fond of chocolate. Breakfast, lunch, and dinner. My salary let me buy it.

By my thirties, I moved slowly, pinched by my own clothing, believing I could not run and that my hip might soon give out entirely, but otherwise I was in perfect health. I told myself my diet could start "tomorrow" because I was "not exactly fat." You see, I did not want to acknowledge I was already fat, both because of cultural prejudices against being fat (it is hard enough dating while transgender without also having an unpopular body size) and because I did not want to stop eating cookies (even if the result would be that I'd walk more easily). I liked to imagine I could carry my goalposts with me so I wouldn't ever find myself having crossed the skinny/fat binary.

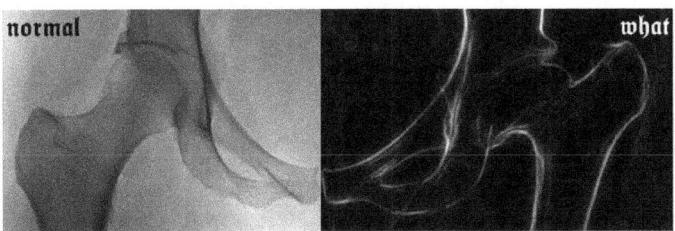

An X-ray of my hips, age 32. The asymmetry is apparent. My pelvis has two sexes (not shown) and two variations on the ball-and-socket joint.

My "hip," in a poetic sense — my pelvis, more broadly — had more to say to me. There had been an orthopedic hip problem, and there was a "transsexual problem." Both problems inhere in my pelvis. There has been a "problem" in my pelvis since infancy. It's a problem zone for me. Early life transmitted to me the belief that my pelvis was inherently defective and destined to be fixed by doctors. It was a preverbal conviction, so no rational argument would dissuade me from it.

The transsexual problem was ongoing, because when surgeons fixed up my chest at eighteen, I didn't immediately arrange for other surgeons to fix up my genitals too.

Jacob wrestled with an angel, and the angel injured him at the "top of the thigh." The meaning has never been clear. Elsewhere in the Bible, that same Hebrew word appears in reproductive contexts. It's either the hip or the genitals. Maybe it's both. After meeting the angel, Jacob limps for the rest of his life, and he fathers no more children.

It's all one pelvic problem. It's all sex. It's all hip.

In *Monty Python and the Holy Grail*, King Arthur and Sir Bedevere encounter The Knights Who Say "Ni!" These oversized, fearsome creatures shriek the lethally annoying word "Ni!" In exchange for shutting up, they demand that Arthur "appease" them with a "sacrifice." They ask for "a shrubbery...one that looks nice...and not *too* expensive." Arthur goes on the shrubbery quest and returns with their laurels. The Knights Who Say "Ni!" envision a second plant placed "slightly higher, so we get the two-level effect with a little path running down the middle," and they send Arthur to find — they pause for dramatic effect — "*another shrubbery!*"

Another surgery it was, for me, then. Finally, at thirty-four, when I had the job and the condo, I arranged for the genital redesign. Though my hip joint was uncomfortable due to the "extra" work it did to carry my "extra" weight, neither my hip nor my weight was relevant to this surgery.

Please understand that, following my chest redesign in my teens, a bit over seven years passed (most of it at university), and then I had my tonsils removed. That was indeed a surgery, but not one I was delighted by. I labored another seven years at an investment company before I was ready for the pelvic redesign. There was more than a bit of Jacob in this. No one was telling me I had to work harder and wait endlessly. I saddled myself with the arbitrary labor.

All decisions for me feel like big decisions. I don't have tattoos mostly because I can't commit. I don't even get haircuts because they temporarily prevent me from getting a different, better haircut. (I was the shaggiest, worst-haircut person of any gender at my office.)

Following through with the surgical decision at age thirty-four was an event for me. I did not care exactly what the result would look like. I knew it would be an innovation, something of a surprise. If it had looked like a bug-eyed garden snail my head might have exploded, but if it had looked like a caterpillar that would have been OK. My feelings about this surgery — similar to the feelings of many people who seek tattoos — were more about the decision and the event than the exact outcome. The physical alteration is about a patch of skin, yes, but more so it's about how that patch of skin is welcomed again into the whole body; how the whole body, in turn, reintegrates with the sense of self; and how the very decision to undergo this process and making or finding oneself available to do it involves a recalibration of whoever you were who hadn't previously decided or been able to undergo it. The result can look like a *khilazon* or whatever.

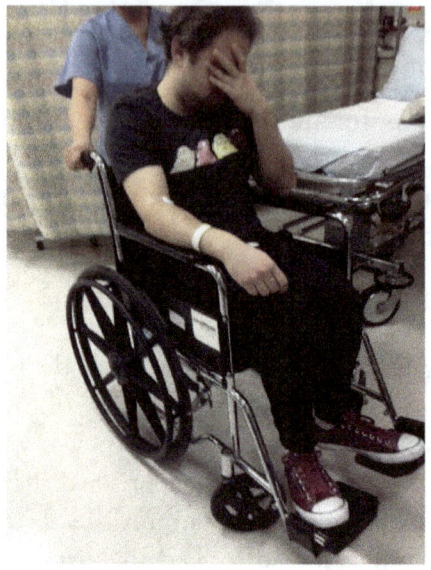

Wheeled out of surgery, age 34. February 25, 2015.

Anyway, I got the Rachel when I was still thirty-four, and, just as I turned thirty-five, I recovered physically. That part was fine. But the physical is not all there is to the process.

when Achilles was a baby, his mother dipped him in the River Styx to make him invulnerable. She held him by the heel so that patch of skin did not receive the boon. The heel tendons we call our Achilles are body parts that, when we least expect it, can rupture.

Let's note that several distressing, frankly bizarre things had happened over the course of my thirtysomething television season, things that only seem to happen to trans people (please take my word for it).

A neighborhood group was concerned about the installation of a large gas pipeline. Some members worried about the climate impact of natural gas (a carbon-based fuel); others worried that the pipeline might explode.

As the volunteer website designer, I cliparted a burning house to serve as our website's main image. I uploaded it in the month I turned 35.

My creation, April 2015

Anything might turn out to be important. Even small events will impact the future in unforeseeable ways. In chaos theory, it's called the "butterfly effect" because the mere flap of an insect's wings can have a downstream result.

When I was 35 and three months, the season finale, an episode I'll call "A Grave Incident," featured a sin of my commission. Several major areas of my life were impacted in ways I was unprepared to handle.

Did the question of God's justice — theodicy — come up? No, I never asked "Why me?" It was obvious that it was me and that I had a hand in it.

The Grave Incident involved other people who I believe would be happier if I do not talk about it.

I did write an essay explaining some of it. It's called "The Trail of His Flames," published in the 2022 anthology *It Came From the Closet*.

Here's a shorter, different explanation:

Moses summoned Aaron to perform hooting, orgiastic blood-magic with fire and guts. Aaron's sons lit a fire of their own in a weak imitation of priesthood and prophecy. They meant well, but oops, they committed some unforgivable sin and God smote them. Moses said: "The boys are dead. Drag them away." And we're all supposed to pretend it didn't happen. Except we read the story aloud in synagogue once a year and propose ideas about what it means.

More prosaically:

A trans man my age and I made a choice that caused our friend, an older trans man, not to speak to us ever again.

Our older friend apostrophized us: "The boys are dead."

On this point, I wrote a book of poems, *Enkidu is Dead and Not Dead / Enkidu está muerto y no lo está*, in 2021.

Some of our worst sins are committed with the best of intentions and sometimes we never figure out what we could or should have done differently. That's the eviscerated goat-heart of the matter.

My inability to deal with stressful events was compounded by overthinking them.

The psychologist Peter K. Chadwick has a personal essay, "Sanity to supersanity to insanity," describing his own "mystico-psychotic crisis." In this essay, he identifies himself as a "man-woman," a "transvestite," a third gender, scorned by his parents and by British society. The problem wasn't him; the problem was others' scorn. It started in 1974 in Bristol, when he was then in his late twenties: "I was being wolf-whistled at in the street, nearly run down by cars full of sneering young men waving limp hands at me, and my friends and girlfriend were suitably informed of my disgusting perverted ways." He blamed his gregarious, gossipy neighbors, who, he heard, had "put a leaflet out on me...with photographs circulating." Of course such harassment would be stressful. The incidents fed into his overthinking and gave structure to it. Predisposed to paranoia anyway, he began to imagine, over the next five years, that these leaflets were achieving an increasing scope and reach from which he had to defend himself. Eventually, he formed the "possibly delusional" impression "that a second leaflet was out on me. I could withstand one, but only just. Two was the end, like doubling the weight a weightlifter has to bear. My sanity was crushed...I started to move from mysticism to madness."[17]

Any number of events might trigger a breakdown, especially if someone is predisposed to such "madness." In Chadwick's case, anti-queer harassment was the trigger, and that specificity matters.

Those who hate us seek to exploit our existing mental vulnerabilities. They cause us to loathe or distrust ourselves in ways we didn't before. Our vulnerabilities increase as we attach new meanings to our wounds.

Like Chadwick, I perceived a particular kind of threat to myself and those around me. Call it the Threat Out of Hell. (It happened simultaneously to the Grave Incident.) The *first* occurrence of the Threat Out of Hell was manageable, but its *second* iteration blew my mind. That I might have misunderstood and fantasized the threat didn't save my mind from blowing.

Pain that we imagine is real pain. In some contexts, words can be deeds (we call them "speech acts"), and I suppose perceptions can become qualities, too. Feeling can become being.

Natalie Eilbert's poem "Imaginal Discs" is titled after the inner parts of caterpillars that contain the biological information for transforming into butterflies. She writes: "A filament / glows like a match absorbing flame, it continues well into / its darkness. One has grown tired of repetition."[18]

Overthinking drove my stress level up. I began to break with reality, "to have a breakdown." I'd always managed situations primarily by thinking about them. But this time, thinking made it worse.

The first symptom was the sealing of my throat. One late evening at the office, I suddenly felt unable to breathe, though I knew it was an illusion because I could speak. "What a queer sensation," I ruminated to a friend on the telephone. "I must be having a panic attack." I stayed at my desk until midnight, afraid to drive home in that condition. I regained my sense of being able to breathe, but my throat remained clenched...for the next year.

I could barely swallow. I had to chew my food until it was liquefied. I'd gag on a grain of rice. It took all of lunch hour to consume a sandwich. A cangue — that is, a yoke of punishment — pulled too tight around the neck perhaps feels like this. The process was disorganized. No matter if I ate, my guts palpitated as if filled with rabid butterflies. Previously, I'd relied on chocolate for a daily chemical lift. Now, in my upset, chocolate could not dent my anguish, and sugar tasted vile. The metabolic sensation of losing weight became comforting, while the sensation of gaining weight was distressing; this was a reversal of what I'd always felt. I wanted to physically dissolve. I became obsessed with drinking water. It was an excuse to jump up from my desk and powerwalk to the office kitchen. Later, on the other end, everything would come out liquid.

My thoughts were a handful of steel bolts in a blender. They never turned off. I wasn't sleeping, either. I was getting as much sleep as the parent of a newborn except that I was alone in my house and it was my own brain waking me up and threatening to bite my own face off with pointy demon teeth. I laid awake shaking, burning calories. Meditate? I could not. Have you ever tried to meditate inside a shrapnel blender? While being mauled by a dog that won't let go? Try meditating when someone is tapping a waltz on your head with a crowbar. Sitting quietly for any number of seconds without BANG BANG BANG BANG BANG see, it is annoying. Sitting without apocalyptic stress would have been the end goal. But how?

I didn't have a first step except for steps. Aerobic exercise was the only thing that eased my mind. I had to go outdoors: Walking. Powerwalking. Running.

As I ate less and exercised more, rather accidentally, I got skinny. In the two or three months following the panic attack, I lost nearly a third of my body weight, at least fifty pounds. My body size approached what it had been at my Bat Mitzvah.

I was of two minds about this. Like most Americans, I had always wanted to be thinner, and now it had happened overnight "without trying" just when the last thing I cared about was impressing anyone with my waistline. My weak hip joint was under less stress and I was aerobically fit, so in those respects I felt physically healthier, but I was swallowing poorly and had insomnia. Mentally, I was not healthy at all, as my own broken brain self-assessed, and that was the determining factor in whether I considered myself "well": no.

I would not have wished this weight loss process on my worst enemy, and I would have taken all the weight back if I could have been happy again. If given the choice, I would have turned the clock back.

The genie always says "Be careful what you wish for," but by the time you feel regret, it is too late.

"a story must be told in such a way that it constitutes help in itself," Martin Buber wrote. "My grandfather was lame. Once...he related how his teacher used to hop and dance while he prayed. My grandfather rose as he spoke, and he was so swept away by his story that he began to hop and dance..."[19]

From the Babylonian Talmud: A non-Jew demanded to be taught the entire Torah with a lesson so brief he could balance on one foot while listening.

Rabbi Shammai swatted him away with a measuring stick.

Rabbi Hillel, however, gave it to him: *Just don't do to anyone else what you wouldn't want them to do to you. That's it. The rest is commentary. Go. Learn.*[20]

Avoid Grave Incidents. That's it. Go. Learn.

The first few times I took a walk to process my feelings about the Grave Incident, I listened to slow instrumentals. My preferred walking speed was a shuffle.

As my mental processing sped up, my music selections sped up with it.

Coming in at 84 beats per minute was Ray Charles singing "Georgia On My Mind."

At 95, Adele sang "Water Under the Bridge."

I walked a little faster.

At 103, the Chainsmokers brought "Something Just Like This."

At 127, Noah Gundersen belted out "The Sound."

This music was too fast to support walking. I was processing my feelings with my body.

At 130, Van Halen had "Jump."

At 146 was Bruce Springsteen's classic "Born to Run."

I was in another zone.

There were more songs. On repeat. To note a technicality, the Chainsmokers and Noah Gundersen were later additions to my playlist; those songs came out a year or two later. I had playlists organized by speed, that's my point. You can do this with your playlists, too. Try varying the speed at which you move your body to vary how you think about your problems. It's a cool trick.

as I rapidly became lighter, I no longer felt my left hip as a constraint, and I moved faster. I needed loud, fast music in headphones, and I would run regardless of the weather or the hour. Midnight. Three a.m. I ran in the freezing rain and ice and in the dark. Out the back door, down the dead-end street, through the cemetery, into the next town.

Running around the edge of Boston. 8 miles per hour. February 25, 2016.

As a teenager I never learned to walk confidently in high heels, but it turns out I can run on snow. I never slipped. Only once I lightly twisted my ankle jumping over a fallen branch.

All the time, my emotions radiated into my body and I felt as if I were being flayed. I considered getting a large tattoo just to experience physical pain that might distract me for a few hours from my thoughts. None of this had ever happened to me before. I didn't have a word for this constellation of symptoms.

Words don't always help, anyway. Many scientific names reassert a diagnosis without explaining it. The satirical example from the 17th century is the *virtus dormitiva*: the name tells us that opium puts people to sleep because it has sleep-inducing properties. Saying it in Latin doesn't mean there's knowledge behind it.

Examples from my life include *congenital hip dysplasia* which means "this baby was born with a crooked hip." They include *transsexual* which means "it has got multiple genders, it changed genders, it discovered and announced its always-authentic gender, or it is doing something along those lines depending on context and who's asking."

These are not explanations.

Miranda Fricker came up with the term *epistemic injustice* in 1999. Specifically, *hermeneutical injustice* is when you can't make sense of your own life because some aspect of your identity is so marginalized that you haven't been taught language to adequately describe your own experiences.

Also, there's *testimonial injustice*: sometimes you report a misdeed or some other bad fire and you aren't believed.

I am white. If I'd been born a different race, my life would have been different. From birth, material situations would have been altered, and I would have developed a different array of reasons and feelings about all sorts of things. Again, the "butterfly effect" means that even a small change can make a major difference.

Living an alternate version of my own life, quite likely I wouldn't have ended up with the exact job I stumbled into in my mid-twenties, so at age thirty-four I would not have had reason to purchase that particular condo in that neighborhood near my office, and furthermore I might have used a word for myself that wasn't *transsexual* and had a different set of lifelong trans friends, and I might have learned different things about how to give and receive mutual aid, and I would not have had the precise series of precipitating events that led to my unique mental breakdown. In an alternate history, one in which I was born as another race, I might still have had a breakdown, but it would have been another flavor. What I had was my own white trans breakdown.

I wrote in "The Trail of His Flames":

> Our world sets itself up so that we do not understand each other, and the suburbs throw their own veil over the "midlife crisis" or "nervous breakdown." A waking nightmare: The system is misbehaving and will never own its shit. If I am not understood, how can I understand myself? If I don't understand others, what do I give and receive? I couldn't pierce the membrane of ignorance and isolation. Even if I had, where

would I have been? Where are we when we "come out"?[21]

Inside the chaos, I was feeling too much private distress to contemplate the extent to which anything (like my race) affected my immediate situation or to have any energy to *do* anything about it. Abstract questions aren't useful as crisis responses. But it was still true that being white did affect my experience. It was an objective truth — about me, about others, about the world — though I didn't actively engage it right then.

Kiese Laymon also ran at night to deal with his work-related stress. His nocturnal exercise began the summer he read James Baldwin's essay arguing that "any real change implies the breakup of the world as one has always known it" and repeatedly read Baldwin's book *The Fire Next Time*. Laymon is a Black man in the United States. Someone reminded him to consider his safety and not run at night.[22]

When I ran at night, the possibility of my being shot or otherwise harassed (seemingly remote as it was) didn't irk me. I wasn't *pondering whether* to take my demons for a walk in the middle of the night; they insisted on being walked, so I *obeyed* them.

Any time I reflect upon my life, my thoughts may be influenced by whiteness. When I don't reflect, white privilege may enable my ignorance or avoidance. Either way, I may fail to come up with good answers.

My first name "Tucker" means "torturer" and my middle name "Brent" means "named by his burns." He is the one who wields the branding iron and is branding himself. An ouroboros. A bad branding experience. Neither is that an explanation, I suppose. It is just announcing what is going on.

Plato proposed in the *Phaedrus* dialogue that it's difficult to navigate our lives given that each of us, as charioteer, drives two horses — Reason and Emotion — with distinct personal horsey agendas. Modern critics note that our reason and emotion are closely linked and usually don't drag us in opposite directions. Those critics are correct, but that's not where I'm going. I'm seeing this from the horses' perspective, too. I don't care if my name is Reason or Emotion; I care that I'm hitched to a cart and a charioteer I cannot see is whipping me. Yes, those are my hooves gathering speed in the dirt, my Reason, my Emotion, but this race is not exactly what I want to be running.

Usually, resting calms stress, but in my case this was inverted. It felt like the moment in Cecil B. DeMille's "The Ten Commandments" when the enslaved woman Yochabel is briefly outpaced by the chain, a near-fatal mistake as the boulder advances toward her trapped body. Taking a nap would have meant letting the great stone overtake me. I would have been dragged. It seemed less painful to obey the forces that were pushing me to move. I zombified myself to keep up the pace. Hence, insomnia.

Three months in, I sought medical help. My physician's assistant spoke to me for a few minutes and prescribed clonazepam (Klonopin). At that time, I still couldn't swallow, so I chewed the pill and took it with water. I habitually did this at night just before turning out the light because the pill immediately put me to sleep. Clonazepam is a benzo tranquilizer. It is supposed to stop convulsions and panic attacks.

I was glad I had started this anti-anxiety pill exactly when I did. Sometimes it takes a while for pills to begin working, and it seemed I'd swallowed the treatment just ahead of my worst symptom as, the very next day,

I began to see myself setting myself on fire.

I doused myself with gasoline and lit a match. This was halfway between a vivid daydream and a hallucination. Call it a specter or phantasm, Latin or Greek for *what I see*.

"Other people surely have hallucinations more potent and persuasive than mine," as I later wrote in "The Trail of His Flames." What's the right word for mine? "How to label things seen-but-not-seen? How to distinguish the sense of watching a movie from watching something in the real world?"[23]

As though someone were flipping on the TV to make me watch it, I was seeing the real world and the movie at the same time. It was only visual, without any other sensations — no sound, no heat. Although it was happening to me in the present moment, I think it used the mechanism of memory, in the way that we can think about past physical pain in some detail without feeling it. I was still able to distinguish fantasy from reality, but the line blurred as my imaginative powers reverted to a more childlike state.

Now, with some years in the rear view mirror, the proper question seems: *Why fire?* When God wanted to get Moses' attention, he lit a bush on fire, and it kept burning. That is the quintessential example of a miracle, the hallmark of some kind of divine intervention. If you see a burning bush, it's supposed to be like getting a phone call from God. What other sign would you be waiting for to prove that it's God? Do you expect God to reveal the correct way to pronounce YHVH, too, before you believe that this is the real deal? Why such skepticism? Why so many demands? Who do you think you are?

No one can see me and live, God says in Exodus 33:20, which is pretty clear. You cannot get too near to the Face of the Presence. But God will show you all kinds of fire.

The fire I saw was clearly important. But exactly what did repeated images of setting myself on fire mean? I didn't know. I wasn't asking yet.

Later, I asked if it meant *I have seen God and He is trying to kill me? I am made in God's image,* b'tzelem elohim, *and I am trying to kill myself?* Or was it some other Jewish metaphor: The sin and destruction of Aaron's sons Nadav and Avihu on the eighth day of the priestly installation ceremony? The vision of Ezekiel in which four winged beings each with four faces emerge from a fiery sky? The lamp oil that unexpectedly lasted eight days in the Hanukah story? The crematories of the Holocaust? One of any number of book burnings and martyrdoms? A witch hunt or inquisition? Was it from another tradition, like the antique Hindu custom of *sati* in which a widow throws herself on her husband's funeral pyre? Or more like St. Spyridon manifesting fire while explaining the Trinity? Abba Lot asking, *How much more spiritual work can I possibly do?* and Abba Joseph responding, *Why not become totally fire?* Something from the news: The suicide of the Tunisian fruit vendor that catalyzed the Arab Spring in 2011? The murder of the Jordanian pilot captured by ISIL in 2015 who placed his hands over his face in prayer as he was set alight? Or something from literature: Stephen King's put-upon Carrie entering a trance state and telekinetically burning down her high school prom? Or film: Freddy Krueger in *Nightmare on Elm Street*, a ghost marked for annihilation by those who believe the legend that fire can destroy him and who surprises us by running up two flights of stairs while he is engulfed in flames?

And why was I drinking so much water?

Arthur Frank gives the example of the child who asks for "one more" glass of water at bedtime. Desire always identifies an object, yet "the object is not what is desired," not *really*, so "the displacements never end: there is no final demand; desire is always wanting more." In general, as we fall asleep, we must agree to temporarily cease desiring anything. This mimicry of death disturbs the child, so they protest by asserting a desire for *something*, because wanting *more* self-confirms they're still alive in the darkness and stillness.[24]

Zombies parody this dynamic. They're supposed to be dead, but they will not stop wandering, hungering, snarling, with no consciousness of what it is that would satisfy them. Watching them, we are sure we'd rather be all-dead than undead.

By thirty-five, I had learned I could get my own glass of water as many times as I liked without asking permission from the boss. One side of my brain said, *"Kill yourself with fire,"* and the other side responded, *"Dispense filtered water into your coffeemug."* More death, more life. More and more and more. It wasn't complex, when I describe it this way; it was just a noisy internal drama for me during business hours in the office kitchenette.

Maybe I was manifesting the image of an *incinerator*, an engine that burned fuel toward a purpose, because I needed to move my life beyond the original trauma that was irking me. I had a huge amount of fuel to burn, but the flame would not extinguish because my personality type was more of a *ruminator*, a goat that stands there chewing and doesn't ever necessarily walk anywhere. I was ruminating on the burning, and I was the fuel being burned. I was burning my own stomach. These hallucinations came unbidden. It was *aish zarah*, the unauthorized fire from *Shemini*, something

I did not ask for. What was I supposed to do: Burn it back with a bigger fire? I was the fuel. The only one who was going to get hurt was me. If I won, I lost. By my own ineptness and inexperience, I made myself the burnt offering.

A character bit from Dale Stromberg's novel *Mæj*: "The only thing I like about you is your fire."[25]

Though these questions come naturally now, the meaning of fire did not concern me in the slightest then. These visions felt real to some degree, they were unpleasant and disruptive to my office workday, and I had pragmatic concerns that I would be susceptible to interpret them as commands. The burning bush exists to get your attention which is a prerequisite for hearing what God is about to tell you to do. If God orders you to lead your nation to freedom, that's nice. If God tells you to do something else, you might be in trouble. I've never heard voices, but I have a strong internal narrator and I didn't want to give it any more ideas.

People who hallucinate and keep their jobs are often labeled as "high-functioning" among those who are mentally ill. I intended to continue to function highly. I just needed to wait for the clonazepam pill to start doing its thing. I was pretty sure it wasn't working yet.

being trans has to do with "upheaval and emergence into a social world with shifting and shifted parameters," writes Hil Malatino. When something happens to us, we need aftercare to heal and emerge into "a radically recalibrated experience of both body-mind and the world it encounters."[26]

Unfortunately, my visions were occurring about every fifteen minutes during waking hours — that is, fifty times a day. I know because I monitored the frequency just as I would have monitored another hypothetical health crisis, like, say, an overactive bladder. One of my bright-idea coping strategies was keeping a journal of the incidents with the hour and minute.

Sun Mon Tue fire log

Why?

Wed Thu Fri fire log

Was I going to do a data analysis?

Sat Sun Mon fire log

(Disingenuous. Arrogant. Attitudes easily leveraged to produce behavior the system recognizes as "working hard.")

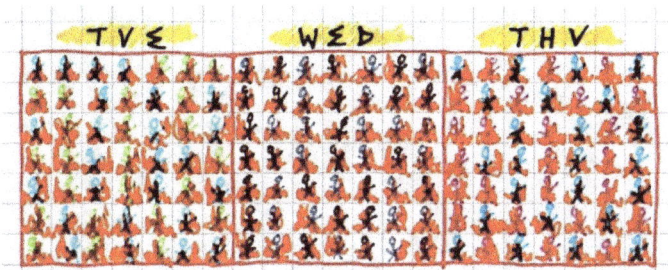

Tue Wed Thu fire log

What I was saying to myself was:

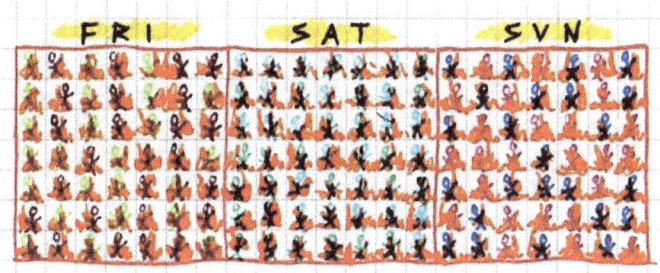

Fri Sat Sun fire log

Obviously I should not be going to work

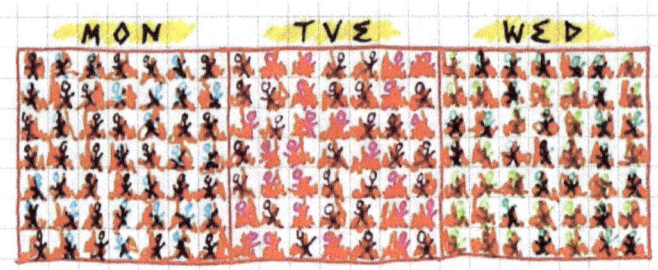

Mon Tue Wed fire log

and I should be getting a lot more help for my problem,

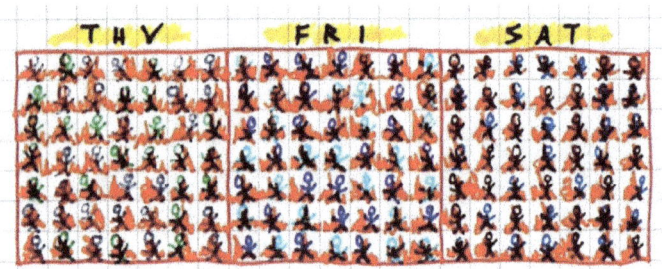

Thu Fri Sat fire log

but I won't. Look how cleverly I mock myself! See how obsessively I assert control!

alatino acknowledges "the standard, hegemonic medical advice given to trans folks in the 1970s, which was to go stealth, blend in, and live as normatively as possible." But is your trans status "irrelevant"? Of course not, and pretending that it is "radically underdetermines the extent to which being trans *continues to matter*, even 'post' transition."[27]

My job at this time was finally shaping into a large career opportunity I'd worked toward for years. Abandoning the income would have posed a problem since I had just become a homeowner. I poured myself into my work, but not in all the manners and dimensions of which I might have availed myself one year earlier. I gave what energy and attention I had. Other parts of me were snatched up in a raging fire. I watched it happen, over and over and over again. What were my career goals? Where did I want to be in five years? Excuse me? The only answer I had was that *three minutes ago I set myself on fire figuratively but not literally, but also sort of literally, and I probably won't set myself on fire really truly literally for the rest of the day as long as I can take two exercise breaks before the sun sets and then run around the cemetery after dark.*

The question of my five-year plan can be answered in a single word. After the answer came to me, I saw Elizabeth Deanna Morris Lakes give the same answer in a poem, "Ashley Doesn't Know": "My boss asked me what my five-year plan was. I said *stay alive,* and she laughed. I wasn't kidding."[28] That is the right answer. *Alive. Five years from now, I want to be alive.* Here's another short phrasing: *I want to last five years.* In the context of running a race, Devin Kelly points out that "the word *last* doesn't just refer to last place, but also refers to *lasting for a long time.*"[29]

because you are mad, you receive truth from a power beyond yourself, but that means your own testimony is a "paradox of witnessing," as Abram J. Lewis put it. Who are "you"? And who's gonna believe you?

Now suppose you become history. Five years have passed. Your scribblings and others' rumors about you are part of what historians call "the archive." It seems "the transgender archive is haunted" because of your madness, hmm? History's "rationalist, positivist, and disciplinary" thinking will reject your "knowledges and experiences," at least the ones that are mad, Lewis says.

But suppose "a truth about a visitation by aliens can be reconstructed as a truth about transphobia." This enables "a new kind of historical recovery."

Other queer people, acknowledging the haunting, might feel a peculiar attachment to your scraps of history while being all the more acutely aware that the true meaning is irretrievably lost. When we "insist upon a haunting," Lewis says, we realize we need "an especially dramatic act of interpretation."[30]

Paraphrasing Lewis's point, Cameron Awkward-Rich says that historians considering "the madness of the transgender archive" must decide "who is granted epistemic authority, under what conditions, and to what effect."[31] In other words, there's always a question of who's allowed to be an expert, of when we'll be ready to recognize their expertise, and of what we're going to do with the mad facts that come out.

"Running around the Cemetery of Grave Incidents after dark." An image I made for the original cover of Bad Fire (2018).

I think some people who worked with me knew, but only unconsciously, that I was running pyrophorically in circles. Sometimes I felt they perceived me as a protective magical animal — maybe a direwolf from *A Song of Ice and Fire*, a mostly huggable furry beast with an occasionally discomforting gaze — but also as a person who might be sick or weak. I felt their skepticism of me; it seemed as if they no longer felt certain whether I gave corporate energy or drained it. These interactions felt the most real. Sometimes I felt effortlessly supernatural, and other times I felt my capabilities were modest, more on a par with an oversized pet that restrains itself to merely *imagine* barking at the mailman (*good dog*).

What was Aaron's job exactly, beyond his job title, "prophet"? What did he do all day? Did he sweep the entrance of the Tabernacle? Don't laugh. Have you ever seen the Tabernacle filled with sand? If not, have you ever considered who keeps it clean? It's hard work to keep the desert out of the Tabernacle. Plus, God dwells in there and sometimes sets people on fire. Aaron does real work. You'll miss him when he's gone.

I was medium-liked, and that was enough for me while I was there. I'm driven to be a people-pleaser but I lack the skills to know what people actually want or how I might give it to them, so I'm fully content when they are medium-happy with me. I was doggedly focused on sweeping the steps of the Tabernacle.

People medium-liked Aaron, God was medium-happy with Aaron, and Aaron was enough. *Dayenu.*

An essential part of being "high-functioning" in an office is hiding vulnerabilities: it's not just about the real work but about the appearance of work. It's about ability and willingness to signal capitalist value. One is expected to be "a worker" in exactly the mold in which the industry would like to use its humans. The key lies in the word "function": "high-functioning" means more machine-like, and "low-functioning" means more human. If I aim for the machine end of the spectrum, then the surface of the water mustn't ruffle. If I tell someone I have a mental illness, I have implicitly raised the topic of whether people are (or should be) machines and reminded others of their mortality, and therefore I will be considered "low-functioning" because I've invoked our shared humanity. In this schema, to have organic batteries is to be low-functioning. It won't matter if I work ten hours a day without a single mistake or delay, solving other people's problems while I'm at it. What will matter is that I will have admitted having an organic brain.

There is not, unfortunately, a professional way to address the uncategorizable persona. The office is a rigid hierarchy, not a community of care. To modify my behavior, my superiors can reach out with carrots, sticks, and a limited number of other tools, but they will not help me with my overthink. They cannot enter my dreams and nightmares and meet me where I am. If I slip from my place in the hierarchy, they will not patch up my angel wings and hand them back to me. Creativity is valued, but sickness or weakness means I will be left to die. In the office, there is no sacred madness, and thus there are no prophets.

Capitalism doesn't know what to do with a wound. Its first inclination is to attack whatever it sees as weak, to root out the infection from the corporate body.

A warning to capitalists: If you attack your direwolf, it will never return to you. If you root me out, I will have to run away.

"There is a Perfect Traveler," Del Samatar and Sofia Samatar wrote in *Monster Portraits*. "He has been running for millennia, light and tireless. In every joint of his body he wears the sign of the wind."[32]

"I will be who I will be," God's voice boomed from the burning bush. Moses could not look at God and had to turn his face away. Or, as the gay chorus sang in *La Cage aux Folles*: "We are what we are." We are flaming queens and this entire performance is an illusion from heels to suspenders.

TUCKER LIEBERMAN

Crouching before running a half-marathon. February 28, 2016.

Cameron Awkward-Rich, in his 2022 book *The Terrible We: Thinking With Trans Maladjustment*, discusses Susan Stryker's 1993 essay "My Words to Victor Frankenstein." He says that essay

> is *mad* in at least four interrelated senses of the word: it records and thinks with the phenomenological experience of breakdown; it privileges felt life over and against

enlightenment rationality; it is, plainly, furious; and it rages, in part, against the regulation of gender variance by psychology, specifically the political, epistemic, and psychic effects of being subject to diagnosis.

Awkward-Rich suggests that we try asking: "What would happen if we thought with these disavowed figures and feelings"? We don't have to *like* these experiences. We can recognize our disorder as unpleasant or perhaps harmful. But that which we've disavowed must have already been part of us. Recognizing this, we may find it fruitful to think with, rather than against, our whole selves.[33]

If anyone saw what was happening to me, I'm pretty sure their understanding was blissfully unburdened by specifics. My problems were disguised. Drowning doesn't look like yelling and waving. The man who appears not to resist the waves is fighting the hardest. A drowning man opens his mouth and lets the water in. The people at the office couldn't see what was happening to me. That is fine, since they would not have rescued me. They might have ritually slaughtered me. Their inattention was quite fair, as neither was I, in retrospect, conscious of their personal struggles.

A recently hired vice president at my company was also a distance runner and asked several times if I wanted to run with him. For most people — those with ambitions to climb the corporate ladder, those for whom running is a healthy hobby — the answer would have been a resounding "yes." And if someone had asked me the previous year (and had I been able to run a mile then), I would have said "yes." This year, I was aerobically fit and running miles and miles, but running wasn't a *hobby* for me. Running was *something else*. My answer was "no," and I couldn't tell this new coworker why.

His question landed on me somewhat like this: *Hey! We both have cholera! Want to plan to go to the latrines tomorrow morning and void our terminally infected colons in unison?* I wanted to say: *I'm not sure what it's like to be you, but my cholera definitely does not work like your cholera.* My brain was going toxic at random intervals during the day and urgently needed to be cleared by a run every couple hours. I didn't plan my run three days in advance as a social activity. This was impossible for me to explain to him. One may choose not to run, golf, or play with the vice presidents, but in any case one is not supposed to *scare* the vice presidents. I could only act oddly withdrawn and unfriendly so that he would stop asking.

This had consequences for me, since this new vice president had been hired to help determine what promotions I and my coworkers would get. The company was in its own prolonged metamorphic phase. We now had what we called "scrum teams." This guy had been scoping me out for a particular lead role, which ordinarily (had I not been insane that year) I would have loved. I had worked for a decade in that general direction, never daring to dream precisely how much I would have valued and aced a role like that. Since I kept blowing him off because my inner demons did not want to do a social 5k with his inner bunnies, he gave the role to someone else.

I was reorganized into a role that was liminal along multiple dimensions. I had to show up for the scrum team's daily meeting without having any clear role within it, and inevitably I was criticized for not actively participating in a role I didn't have — like a Little League right fielder who is criticized for *standing and waiting* when that is the whole point of right field, and then in addition the team captain expects that same player to interdimensionally and trans-loyally stand in multiple places and occasionally *hit* the ball while the other team is at bat, then *catch* the ball before the pitcher ever made a move, and then the captain tells the player *don't back down* but also *don't start a fight*. See what this is a recipe for. It's like we're watching our own baseball game on TV. Before the commercial break, someone will be yelling.

I don't mind being liminal; it's the only way I know how to be. But it takes more energy to accomplish a task if I have to leverage myself across different astral planes and no one can see what I am doing. Once I'm playing interdimensional baseball, I'm stuck there, because asking to be given a comprehensible and non-contradictory role will be perceived as an inappropriate request to reduce my workload. Trying to clarify my needs will make it worse, as no one is prepared to brook an honest discussion when my reasons will distill to "because I'm hallucinating setting myself on fire." So there I remain, doing the same old thing in all the fields at once.

My mind was that blender full of steel bolts, gearing up hallucinations just as I started clonazepam, and with extraordinary patience, I waited for the new medication to start working. I set myself on fire fifty times a day during the three weeks I took the pill.

...*Wait*. What if the pill is not the cure, but the—

It had been a good idea to try a pharmaceutical, but *this* pill caused the worst ideas I've ever had. As I said, the worst sins sometimes result from the best intentions.

Clonazepam may fix some brains, but it was very bad for mine. It was a strong, fast-acting sedative for me at bedtime, but at sunrise I awoke feeling I'd poured gasoline inside the blender, loose shrapnel still rattling inside, now with sparks flying everywhere. This effect is known, it turns out. A few people who take clonazepam become hallucinatory, uneasy, psychotic, suicidal. It helped me sleep, but otherwise it didn't do much for my anxiety, plus it added distressing CGI effects.

The day after I started the pill, the visions started; the day after I stopped the pill, the visions stopped and never returned. Well, the cause had become clear, and the solution was clear too. Unfortunately, it had taken me three weeks to figure out.

Quitting the bad pill meant I wasn't pouring any more gas into the blender. From that point on, any thoughts of fire were normal memories, daydreams I had control over, "my" thoughts, not emergency alerts beginning *"We interrupt this broadcast..."* from the Central Government of We Set Things On Fire Right Now. That was a good start.

The overall anxiety blender, however, was still powered on. It was just that now I was no longer taking a pill that made my life worse.

All assessments are challenging. Whatever tool you use will find what it's designed to find. "Temperature is not as simple a concept as it seems," Elisa Gabbert says. Temperature, which is neither heat nor energy, "is what thermometers measure."[34]

There was an undefined, perhaps hourly recurring suicidal impulse that felt as though I were hitting myself in the head with a garden trowel. I was still skinny, still taking frequent jogging breaks (long-distance, when possible, round the clock) to hold myself together, still sweating through the armpits of my office shirts, and I couldn't sleep well. Sleep was the one good thing clonazepam had done for me, and I was no longer taking it. I avoided travel because I couldn't sit still in a vehicle for more than a couple hours.

I believed I was constructively "processing" my thoughts, but I was making a lot of stuff up. "When intense events happen in close proximity to one another, the human mind often tries," Naomi Klein writes in On Fire, "to draw connections that are not there, a phenomenon known as apophenia."[35]

And why do we draw false connections? Maybe because we feel ambivalent toward all the dark matter of which we are ignorant. We run hot and cold because we don't know if what we desire or fear is really desirable or frightening, and our changing feelings expose our ignorance to ourselves, too. We fantasize to provide answers so we'll know where we stand. Lauren Berlant identified "misrecognition (*méconnaissance*)" as "the psychic process by which fantasy recalibrates what we encounter." We "project qualities onto something so that we can love, hate, and manipulate it."[36]

Projection and fantasy are always false, then, or they're true only by accident — they're bullshit, if not lies. We're self-soothing by telling ourselves we know what we want. When the process goes awry, we're left with a continually shifting set of values and symbols, and we lose control of the story.

During this era of anxiety, I wrote voluminously, and it was longer, denser, and weirder than anything I'd written before. My handwriting worsened.

I still could barely swallow and didn't like to eat much of anything, especially sugar, but there was one exception. On the weekends, even in the winter cold, I liked to run two miles to a gelato store, drink a mildly flavored gelato milkshake, and run back. The net calorie gain was small and didn't help me put on any weight, but it still felt comforting. This was a medical clue. So interested was I in developing my elaborate fantasy system that I didn't spot this useful data point until much later.

I often delay decisions because action manifests a particular future, closes off possibilities, and denies further rumination. Out of the same sense of future-scarcity, I did not set myself on fire in the actual world, since it occurred to me that I could only do it once and I was more interested in continuing to imagine dozens of ways in which I might do it. I wanted to determine what others might see and what they might understand from it.

"Everyone's holding up their phones to take pictures" of a California wildfire, says the narrator of Sam Sax's novel *Yr Dead*, "instead of running to find a place they can breathe…what supersedes the desire to survive is the desire to look, to document the world as it leaves us."[37]

Even if some pills have injured you, going without any medicine at all isn't necessarily the answer. When Peter Chadwick slipped into what he calls "madness," within weeks he threw himself in front of a bus, was diagnosed with "schizoaffective psychosis," and was given a maintenance medication that worked for him. He links "mysticism and psychosis," favors "an alternative view of reality" that he sees as valuable and urgent to explore, and yet says he also takes his meds.[38] This is a coherent choice. Just because it is good to explore the woods does not mean you should wander in with no water bottle and no expectations of returning.

Soon I was willing to try a different pill, and this one made all the difference: a low dose of trazodone, an antidepressant that affects serotonin. I took it daily before my last run of the evening, giving myself just enough time for a ten-minute sweaty jog around the neighborhood to stabilize my thoughts before the pill kicked in and I woozily walked back up to my apartment for bed. It worked for me. It quieted my thoughts enough to give me a chance at a full night's sleep and to have a more ordinary range of thoughts and feelings the next day. It helped me focus on work and other things I needed to do. I often wanted to double up on the trazodone pill to smooth the path — doing so would have anyway amounted to a more common dose — but I held myself to the low dose, trying to see how much my brain could kickstart on its own.

I took trazodone for six months. It probably saved my life. By the end of that period, I was beginning to swallow food a bit better, and I finally believed myself able to get through the day without the chemical assistance. I staggered days with and without the pill. The days I resolved to go without it felt hard, I mean Garfield-hates-Mondays miserable, but I had faith in myself that I could get a grip and "hold it together" without medication. I did, just barely. I stopped taking the pill altogether and never resumed it.

The office was a high-stress environment. Thinking about my recovery from anxiety, it was helpful to have a familiar office to go to and a job to focus on, but it was not helpful to have so much stress, which may have fed my anxiety in the first place.

I'm not sure how I could have asked for help at work. *This company needs to dial down the stress level so the employees don't die* would not have been what bosses call "an actionable request." Long weekends could have been granted to me here and there, but to show proper gratitude I would have needed to return the following week entirely fixed in mind and body. They send a worker home to get a good night's sleep and a good day's movie marathon and expect this prescription will make "it" better. They anticipate the mystery of sleep fixing the mystery of whatever-the-problem-was.

The balance of work-and-rest has been challenging for thousands of years, and workers have always been blamed for not achieving that balance. "Do your work during the six weekdays," God says in Exodus 31:15, but "whoever does any work on Saturday shall be put to death." That's about as clear as it can be. *We will kill you if you don't rest properly.* But also, the boss sometimes needs me to work on Saturdays, so there's that.

Rest. For a whole weekend! Then be fully-already-rested. They don't understand the magnitude of what they're asking for. They may as well invite me to spend the weekend getting a master's degree and having a baby so I can look more effective, happy, and normal when I return on Monday.

I knew it was impossible. They weren't really asking me to execute a transformation; they wanted me not to need a transformation in the first place, and they wanted me not to be transforming in ways unrelated to work. They wanted me to live more like everyone else and lose my "lonely homosexual" visage. They didn't literally need me to get a good night's sleep. They wanted to not feel guilty that I was queer and unhappy.

Anyway, sleeping peacefully was exactly the skill deficit at issue and it would take years before I'd have that skill again. These smoldering trash fires were not going to be put out in a day, nor even in a year.

In the '80s, my family had a voice-controlled, battery-operated toy called Petster. It looked like a Muppet cat with a springy tail. When I clapped my hands, Petster zoomed down the hallway carpet, twirled on the kitchen floor, flashed red pupils, and meowed like a dying R2D2.

"When you first turn me on, my eyes flash evenly at a medium rate (about 2 flashes per second). This tells you I am in my Ready-to-Play mode. From this mode I can be given 5 distinct commands: 1. Come Here 2. Go Away 3. Purr 4. Obey 5. Go Play"

– The Petster Manual, "Owner's Manual and Training Guide," Axlon, 1985.

While Asleep, I am only drawing a tiny amount of electric current, so you can leave me turned ON most of the time. As a matter of fact, I can be awakened to play after being Asleep for over 3 weeks.

"While Asleep, I am only drawing a tiny amount of electric current, so you can leave me turned ON most of the time. As a matter of fact, I can be awakened to play after being Asleep for over 3 weeks."

– *The Petster Manual,* "Owner's Manual and Training Guide," Axlon, 1985.

Today, the bosses want Petster to go home, recharge its batteries, and come back to the office, but they don't want it to do any of the annoying Petster tricks. What, exactly, do they want from Petster? What did they ever expect it to do?

It seemed to me I was the only employee who had a nervous breakdown. This was a barrier to bringing up the subject. *Why is it only the queer who sets himself on fire?* was my judgment against myself.

(It is implausible that I have cornered the market on nervous breakdowns. I have since gathered more information about who amongst my coworkers had their own struggles.)

Things happen. There's a glitch in the Matrix. No one else notices it. It looks like a regular rabbit hole to them, and they step around it. I fall through it.

If queer people do suffer higher rates of mental illness, maybe that's because of stigma against queerness, of arguments built of nonsense and circles, of gatekeeperish rules about our bodies, of campaigns to erase our documents and keep us out of public bathrooms. This kind of chronic stress fuels mental illness. It is cultural and environmental. Maybe it's not so much inherent in the queer person but in the way that we are queered by others.

Or maybe it is inherent in us. But how do we see it for what it is and own it, especially when we are shamed and threatened over it?

Another reason why trans people might be prone to weird vision is *I don't know and neither do you.*[39]

"*Vos mir zeinen zeinen mir, ober Yiden zeinen mir,*" a folk song has it. "We are whatever we are, but we are Jews."[40]

Usually, we aren't seeking our true selves (which we already inhabit, like it or not) but are trying to pronounce our own names. The game show host will not give us credit for the answer unless we pronounce it correctly. The riddle ultimately dissolves in the pronunciation.

R abbis sometimes say that the Torah addresses every possible subject. I heard this when I was growing up. Does the Torah have a story on suicide, though? That's a tricky one to find.

It's Nadav and Avihu. They died by suicide. When God burned them up — that was suicide. I do not mean that they engineered a "suicide-by-cop" (a deliberate provocation of a lethal response) nor that they "should have known better." I mean, more simply, that they died by their own hands.

This interpretation explains why Moses ordered their bodies removed from the camp and why he warned Aaron not to ritually grieve them. It may be historically consistent with the treatment of people who die by suicide. See, for example, the advice in the 16th-century *Shulchan Arukh* not to eulogize or mourn people who die this way (*Yoreh De'ah* 345:1).

Does it puncture the theory to note that, according to the text, the deadly fire came from God? Yes, if we understand God as a separate person in physical space. But is that where God really is? Where is God ever except inside people's imaginations? If we understand God as an idea, a feeling, a presence people encounter within themselves, then what comes "from God" really emanates from a mysterious part of ourselves.

If we understand "the divine" as internal, the unauthorized sacrifice offered by Aaron's sons could have been themselves. They chose to die, sacrificing themselves to an inner voice. When God kills men, that means they kill themselves.

Nadav and Avihu were priests-in-training, ordered to kill an animal. They offered wrong fire to God. Fire from God's presence burned them up. *They were the sacrifice.* They were not punished for sacrifice with death; rather, they were punished for death with ignominy. Their suicide was rejected and made taboo.

The English mathematician Alan Turing was punitively sentenced to chemical castration for his sexual relationship with another man. He died by suicide.

"I wish people who believe in God," the fictional Turing says in Will Eaves' novel *Murmur*, "could believe in him a little less fervently — could see him as a metaphor for the boundedness of our physical existences and the problem of the mental, which is physical, too, but perhaps in a way we don't understand." The body-mind isn't a binary.

The story of Nadav and Avihu records two suicides. Perhaps a murder-suicide, or a suicide and an accident; the level of premeditation isn't described. The general idea, though, is that sometimes a person's brain burns up and kills them.

Saying that two guys approached God strangely and that God set them on fire is pretty much saying their brains glitched out and they killed themselves.

Blaming them for impurity and putting a taboo on the whole story makes it extra clear.

Here, human transgression and divine anger are each other's shadows. Bad fire becomes worse fire.

Were they in an altered state? The term is inexact. There is no *state*, and *altered* and *unaltered* isn't a real binary. A brain floats in a chemical bath inside the skull. Its condition is therefore both natural and chosen, and none of us can detach our brain from its environment of food, water, air, microparticles. There is no default state. To paraphrase Erik Davis, we drift in and out of zones of experience in which we perceive differently, but no one type of awareness is the true awareness.

Davis goes on to emphasize that this reality is not solely private. Part of its meaning is in how we relate to others:

> Instead of framing ASCs [altered states of consciousness] as discrete states that are internal to an individual's skull, [Robert] Wallis instead underscores their *transitive* character, their reaching out towards objects and other beings. In this sense, ASCs [reinterpreted as *adjusted styles of communication*] establish themselves *relationally*, in conjunction with a lively and interactive Beyond, some inside-outside dimension of reality that seems to have something to say.[41]

Not everyone who has suicidal thoughts will die. Sometimes those thoughts tread a line of the literal and figurative. We think about physically dying, but instead we may die to ourselves and go on physically living. We remain in relation.

Andrew Harvey once said: "When the whole of your being, when your time comes for you to be killed by the divine, you will surrender to mystery, and the real divine consciousness can come through you."

To which Zenju Earthlyn Manuel adds that this event includes the realization that neither you, nor the divine force that runs through you, is an object. You will not have a choice in this realization. You dwell in darkness and light, gain new perspective about darkness and light, and revalue the roles of darkness and light. "The fire, filled with smoke and unclear light, still illuminates what is ancient in us, in the sanctuary, and in the world," says Manuel. "We might tremble and run from the dark, thinking that it is the opposite of the light we are seeking. When we do so, we are running from light as much as from darkness."[42]

The story of Nadav and Avihu also reflects how people who are currently in non-suicidal zones of experience may react to others who are in suicidal zones.

Some "inspirational" and "leadership" coaching, the way I receive it, boils down to this: *Boost all your good qualities and get rid of all your bad qualities!* A simple formula. But can you do that? No.

Think about a battery: One side is labeled "positive," the other "negative." That doesn't mean one side is good and the other bad. Electricity is the flow of charges. You need a positive and a negative side or you don't have a flow of charges, which means your Petster won't spin. It's not that the "negative" side of your battery is actually "good," nor would it be "bad" to get rid of it. The issue is that you *can't* cut it out. The electrons build up in one area and the charges are lopsided so they rescramble themselves. The electrons have to be inside the battery. They'll move around, but you can't just "not have them." Their meaning and value is always changing. That's the magic of electrical power. A battery without a negative side isn't a battery. At least, it's not like any battery I've ever put in my Petster.

BAD FIRE

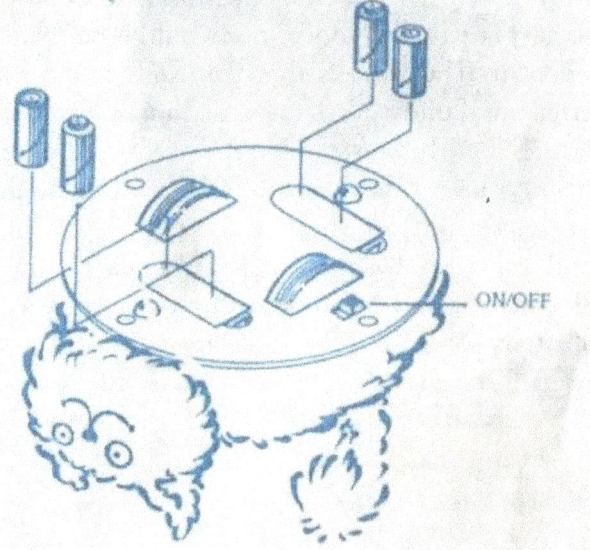

Turn me over, and make sure my ON/OFF switch is set to the OFF position. Open the battery compartments, and install the batteries, being careful to match the plus (+) and minus (−) signs on the batteries and in the compartments.

"*Turn me over, and make sure my ON/OFF switch is set to the OFF position. Open the battery compartments, and install the batteries, being careful to match the plus (+) and minus (-) signs on the batteries and in the compartments.*"

– The Petster Manual, "Owner's Manual and Training Guide," Axlon, 1985.

It's the same with *yin* and *yang*, as I understand it: the pull and push, feminine and masculine. It's not as though there's a *yin* pile and a *yang* pile and you can cleanly subtract from one pile while adding to the other. It's not as though each of us has static values like a Dungeons and Dragons character (Masculine +4, Feminine +6) that tell us the probable outcome of any battle. All our being is in the same writhing pile.

In the Navajo (Diné) language, as explained by Navajo Two-Spirit person Anthony Johnson,

> *nádleeh* means 'ambient being.' If you think about energetic forces inside a body, it's like these two forces that oscillate back and forth. It's not just male, it's not just female — it's male-female, back and forth, all the time.[43]

Our health is like this, too. We don't have a binary healthy-or-sick status. It can't be represented as a "static" image in which "light is separated from dark," says Arthur Frank in *The Wounded Storyteller*. It would be better represented as an animation in which "one shape is constantly in process of becoming the other."[44]

We have multiple guiding hands on our shoulders, and each of our attributes is nothing more than the way we interact with what's around and within us. Even rocks interact in their own way, if you're willing to perceive it; kick a rock, and the rock kicks back at your foot by not letting you through. Everything rubs up against everything else. You drink and sometimes you say "the water is wet" and sometimes you say "my throat is wet." The ocean wave is pushing and pulling, coming into being and disappearing, all at the same time. You can divert the wave to some degree, but you can't make it so that it only ever gets bigger and never disappears. That's not what a wave is. It isn't the quantity of water nor the shape it takes, and it isn't endless growth. It is made of time. It is change. Its weakness and its negativity are part of it. One wave will disappear while forming another wave. It is made of growth-and-disappearance. Its emergence foreshadows its end. What you see as its being is its nonbeing.

You can stand in its path. Now you are the one who is wet. Now you are the body who did not let the water pass through you.

Thinking of cycle, motion, and moving images, I visualize a duck floating on the rippling water. The duck advances slowly, yet its webbed feet paddle furiously beneath the surface. It is cycling its ideas, concealing its plans, unconsciously or deliberately. It is moving even if someone standing on the shore perceives it to be motionless.

When water boils, it is transitioning from one state to another. When you boil water, you are asking for the water to move. If bubbles aren't making and unmaking themselves, and if they don't travel upward as they unmake themselves, the water isn't boiling. When it boils, what is the "it" that is boiling? The liquid? The vapor?

A God who gives us anything at all is a God who gives us things we like and things we don't like. A God who rewards us is also a God who punishes us. If we sit on a see-saw with God, we are not going to swing infinitely upward into delirious joy, heavy as God may be on the other end. For if God has all possible powers, God is both infinitely heavy and infinitely light. And the see-saw is designed to move.

You are not the same person you were five years ago. Neither does your femininity or masculinity remain identical to whatever you once believed it to be. You're aging. The world is turning.

Everything you care about is a moving part relative to something else.

Your attention. ("A person's attentional style doesn't operate in a vacuum, but in the larger context of his or her other traits," said Winifred Gallagher.[45])

Your resource-grabs. ("As long as some can talk only about their materialism, others can talk only about their survival," said Jim Wallis.[46])

Your trans friends. (Within trans communities, it's hard to distinguish "the roles of carer and recipient," said Hil Malatino. There are "kinds of mutual traumatic resonance that circulate between trans subjects involved in acts of caring," and "we are often triggered by one another in the act of caring but nevertheless *need* one another."[47])

Your adjustment and your maladjustment. (There is "a version of *trans* that thinks with, rather than against, what I call *trans maladjustment*," says Cameron Awkward-Rich.[48])

Your left hip and your right hip.

It's all an ongoing balancing act while you move forward. All of it.

earlier, I mentioned that the flavor of my mental illness was an artifact of my whiteness. I ran around my city neighborhood at night, free from an expectation of being policed.

Imagine that all neighborhoods were reasonably safe, that no one was policed just for existing, and that our skin colors did not determine who among us could safely run at night.

In that reality, we might be more interested in which neighborhoods had *privacy*: whether you could run at night and be wholly ignored (as was my experience) or whether your neighbors would notice your suddenly altered behavior, care about it, and offer some form of support (if only a cup of herbal tea and a chat).

In this case, when considering where you want to live, a "less private," more socially connected neighborhood might be "safer" because your neighbors would kindly interfere if your brain ever started to eat itself. How many of us would choose to live in a more socially connected place, a place where we could plan communal strategies that would actually help each other? How many of us would have less severe manifestations of mental illness if our neighborhoods affirmed life?

To affirm life would entail, of course, not being racist. And in our actual world, not being racist involves actively fighting racism.

We have to envision the change if we want to make new realities and unmake old ones. Baldwin said: "Any real change implies the breakup of the world as one has always known it."[49]

a "complex self," as the psychologist Mihaly Csikszentmihalyi wrote in *Flow*, successfully combines two drives. "Differentiation implies a movement toward uniqueness, toward separating oneself from others. Integration refers to its opposite: a union with other people, with ideas and entities beyond the self."[50]

the company might have granted me medical leave if I'd asked, but I suppose I knew that even a long leave would not have been long enough. I was either in the game or out of it. I stayed in the game for a while and continued to get better, slowly. I did not really heal until I left the game and stayed out.

The self-consuming snake is in action. Its tail is impaled with its own venom. It doesn't take a break to meditate. It has to find a way out of its own head.

We will be happy when we are able to meditate. It will take two or three years. We will have to move to a quieter place before we can sit.

In Plato's allegory of the cave, people walk past a fire, producing shadows on the wall. Chained prisoners see the shadows but cannot reposition themselves to see the people who are causing these images. The fire isn't at fault; it's just a source of light. That the prisoners see only shadows is a problem of their perspective. They will never see the source of the shadows until they find a way to move.

m ad vision is a valid approach to life. It's an alternate sense-making engine. It's valuable and rare. To some extent, it is whatever we make of it or whatever we're willing to take from it. Of psychiatric events about which we do not feel "distress," Esmé Weijun Wang notes that "a symptom might be a welcome attribute, and therefore an ability."[51]

But we often *do* feel distress. Madness is a lot less comfortable than intellectual routes to knowledge, and it's not quite a privilege.

I would say the same of my trans status. Considered as a social deviance (which is part of my experience of being trans), being trans imparts new ways of perceiving, which confers advantages and disadvantages.

And when I report what happens, the so-called delusional accounts I give while being so-called insane are, as Abram J. Lewis says, "by no means easily disentangled from accounts of living in a violently transphobic capitalist order." Avery Gordon (as quoted by Lewis) tells us that "a repressed or unresolved social violence is making itself known," that there is "more than one story at a time," and that the ways we take in information "are anything but transparent and referential."[52]

I told my boss I wanted a newfangled job title like the ones they dole out in Silicon Valley: *information architect*, please, or else *thought leader, evangelist, demigod*. He said: *No, but you can be a regular prophet, that sounds good to us*. It's always about their profit. That's how I came to be called *product manager*.

Employers may be skeptical of mad skills, and for good reason. Hallucination of violent images does not generally recommend a candidate for any job. Madness isn't a capitalist value. I'd call it a "spiritual" or perhaps "prophetic" value if I liked those concepts, but I'm a bit too atheist for that.

Nonetheless, despite its non-capitalism, madness can have positive outcomes in the office. Dealing with mental illness is a crucible for developing uncommon endurance. That affects who I am at work and who I am in the rest of my life. When I hallucinate suicide by fire one thousand times in rapid succession and don't act on it because I am busy doing something important for the company, I evidence a kind of loyalty that Human Resources won't find again just by placing a classified ad. This flavor is rare, difficult to deliberately leverage, and generally not for sale.

Madness makes us miserable, yes? It yields us to our conviction of catastrophe and to our chaos of character, the existential disorder called *kilkul* in Hebrew[53] or *gibel* in Russian.[54] *Zuul* is how the gatekeeper demon in *Ghostbusters* pronounces its name from its hiding place in the fridge; it isn't anything you can sort out. The problem is not what the demon is saying but that you hear it speaking at all. Labeling yourself as "having a breakdown" and declaring yourself a cliché for having a demon in your fridge might seem to be putting your foot down, but merely protesting "I don't want this" doesn't get rid of the demon in the fridge.

Madness brings us "pain, terror, destruction, and abjection," but, La Marr Jurelle Bruce points out, capital-R "Reason" does the same when it is used to justify violence (as it frequently is). He's talking about the sort of "reason" fetishized by old-guard philosophers who pretend that only some humans achieve rational thought. These philosophers imagine certain categories of humans when they assert ability and inability. They're elitists whose philosophical product is oppression.[55] So if we still have a place for self-anointed "rational thought" despite the widely varying results of this so-called muse named Reason, why can't we also appreciate mad experience? Why would we greet the apparent "madperson" with more suspicion than the apparent "rationalist"? Who and what are we valuing?

I remain perplexed by professional self-evaluations that require me to grade my own efforts of the past six months on a scale from One to Five. I do not like that idea at all. Obviously I am working as hard as I can.

Obviously the department's successes and failures reflect on our teamwork, not only on whether I (as an individual) stayed eight hours or twelve hours and whether I swallowed a pill, though how I take care of myself does impact my ability to contribute to a team. What I think of myself is not separable from what others think of me, at least if the bosses are asking me how I feel our group project is going. If the bosses want to understand the teamwork, they should ask the group members to discuss the group dynamics. When instead they ask me to grade myself, they are just asking me to reveal my wounds, and I know that their response will only be: *Fix it or die*. It's bullying, really, isn't it. *One through Five. Fix it or Die.* That's not how life comes to any of us.

There was darkness and God said, "Let there be light." There was smoke and simultaneously there was fire. We exist in ways that are counterproductive, scary, or annoying and, on the other side of the coin, we are useful, brilliant, and proud. It would be nice to think that the "real" me is wholly good, capable, and visionary and that temporary insanity worked against my best qualities. I'd like to imagine that I would have performed better at my job if I hadn't been mentally ill. But I don't know that there could have been a truer, purer me who aced my life and went to the "next level."

First, on principle, I don't think there can be a "get better" psych pill to make me more useful to my boss and simultaneously more authentically myself.

"Do more" and "be more" often ride a seesaw, magnifying and lessening inversely. One can begin "being" one's true self and end up "doing" quite a lot, but what one does with one's true self may not be what the boss asked for.

Second, there was no counterfactual me who was never sick, and I have no reason to think that alternate reality was a possible one. Maybe I didn't have a personal "next level"; maybe I was as skillful as I could get. To look at that same point from another angle, maybe I maxed out this level and the way to the next level was not merely typing the spreadsheet faster but entering a wholly new life stage, butterfly-style.

The caterpillar hears the roar and the crunch of its own leaf-appetite. At first, this is background noise. One day, the caterpillar feels less hungry, and it notices the noise of its own chewing and is maddened by it.

The caterpillar asks its God a wordless question: "???"

God says: *"It depends what you're hearing. If it's an alarmingly loud whine that only gets worse when you lean into it as if you're flooring the gas pedal while the transmission is in neutral, then, yes, it's time."*

The caterpillar asks: *"What's a gas pedal? What's a transmission? What's time? I have only ever listened to my own thoughts. This metaphor is beyond my comprehension."*

God says: *"It's not exactly a metaphor. Just wait."*

The caterpillar's time is up for eating leaves. It listens to its hormonal prompts and forms a cocoon to change into a butterfly. If the caterpillar is hormonally disregulated and doesn't do this, it will dehydrate and not be part of the world anymore. It can't eat its way out of this predicament. Chewing and swallowing faster won't solve the problem. You can't give it a ten-thousand-dollar raise and expect more caterpillaring out of it. It is going to change or die. It embarks on the grand passage. This is how it becomes a wise elder and not just a child who ate enough to reach an adult weight.

"I have news for you," says God.

"What now," says the butterfly-in-progress.

"You're the khilazon," says God.

"No way. Can't be. I'm not a snail," says the butterfly-in-progress.

"You're not a caterpillar anymore nor a butterfly yet either. What's your point?" says God.

"I haven't got a shell," says the butterfly-in-progress.

"You do so. You are sleeping snugly in it. I see you from the inside and from the outside. And your blood is indigo. It's you. It was you all this time," says God.

When the caterpillar finally changes, when the butterfly emerges, it might not look like its boss. Why should it? Do zoo animals ever change to look like their zookeepers?

If I bring my caterpillar self to another office, the story will repeat. There, I will once again run around the office shouting deep logic from an astral plane. They will gradually tune into what I am saying and pay me what I am worth. They will never make me a vice president, however, because I won't go jogging with them, or golfing, or whatever it is they do to ritually upgrade themselves in that religious system. I am not a vice president. I am a transsexual. If they are not doing the work even to see me, still less will I make an effort to ape them. I can be a little bit performative, but I cannot live out a wholly other destiny. No matter how many years I contemplate weaving the cocoon, never will I emerge looking like my boss. I will only ever look like myself. Admitting this respects my boss's humanity as well as my own.

I am what I am; there is no other version of me. Past, present, and future instantiations, yes, but I can't veer radically off-script. And there can only be one me at a time. If someone happens to spot my past and future roles and likes them, that's great, but I can't play my own multiple roles simultaneously. I can't go back to what I used to be, and I can't arrive at my next stage before I get there. That's time-travel.

Being oneself right now means letting go of ideas about oneself. Ideas never match what really exists. The metaphor belongs to past or future, and the present is always slipping through our fingers. There's nothing to be grasped.

"*OK, so I'm the khilazon,*" says the khilazon.

"*Yep,*" says God.

"*What am I supposed to do now?*" asks the khilazon.

"*Nothing,*" says God.

"*But what's my purpose?*" says the khilazon.

"*Well, erm, you might not like it,*" says God.

"*Nu?*" prompts the khilazon.

"*It's really very smashy and it might hurt,*" says God.

"*Oh no,*" says the khilazon.

"*Don't worry too much. Just hope that the Messiah doesn't come anytime soon,*" says God.

An "extractive" approach will squeeze more product from the Earth, but the thing we most want isn't a product. While we wait for the Messiah, we may as well learn something from the waiting. If we smash snails to seek out the khilazon with its blue glands, our thinking is narrow, and we're missing an opportunity. Blue may be anywhere. Blueness will reveal itself, and there may be no way to speed up the process.

"A Caterpillar Chewing a Weed Leaf Wonders if He'll Ever Become a Butterfly" is the title of a poem by Elaine Wang. She questions: "What does it mean to carry / your destiny in your body" and "have to destroy yourself" to unbox that destiny?[56] The meaning of your life right now is that it will change. You will change. Your body is a container, but you can't open it violently. It might open itself violently. You have to wait. If your body happens to burn up, what's inside will be released. If something happens on its own, it may happen for its own reason, and you can let it happen. There is nothing to be gained from forcing it.

T hird — still regarding whether I'm an inadequate example of my best true self — I don't regret my constraints or the outcome. Maybe I would have performed worse at work if I hadn't been sick. I can't know that madness didn't somehow help me or save me from a worse fate.

When you play a game of chance, you may grumble about rolling a 3 and complain you could've gotten a 6, but equally you could be grateful you didn't roll a 1. If you turn left and are hit by a car, you may wish you'd turned right, but how do you know that, in that alternate scenario, you wouldn't have been hit by a truck?

When you accept that certain elements aren't under your control, you may shift focus to examine what you do control. What role has your character played in your catastrophes? You may wish you'd been better, kinder, stronger, more patient and flexible. And yet — you weren't those things. Reality was not how you imagine you would have liked it. You could not have reacted to stress in a better way because you were the sort of person who reacted exactly the way you did in that scenario. You can improve yourself in the future, but you can't go back and be someone else in the past. And maybe there was a reason that you were the way you were then. Maybe it was good that you were. The outcome is that you've arrived at this reflection today. This is an opportunity to be who you should be right now.

Something in me pulled me through the toughest slog even as it simultaneously kicked my shins in the direction of the Underworld. The exact way it happened was unique to me. Maybe this was the only way it could have been. I am no one other than this.

I neither claim nor receive credit for it.

"What merit has fire for burning," the 4th-century archbishop Gregory Nazianzen asked, "since it is its nature to burn?" He was speaking specifically of castrated men. He said he doesn't give them spiritual credit for celibacy if they couldn't have been libidinous anyway. He awards spiritual credit only for acts of willpower. "I demand something else from the eunuchs," Gregory said.[57] He was the boss, and the eunuchs may have had to render up something upon his demand.

I don't care what Gregory would have thought of me being trans. Each of us can decide what's important to us. We can listen to our own natures.

Genders have secret meaning that can't be performed upon the boss's request. Saying "I demand" is a surefire way not to get the secret meaning.

I demand something else from the trans. I can demand it from my own trans if I am trans. But it will not listen even to my trans command. It is too trans to obey.

I don't just *see* the burning bush. I *am* the burning bush. I contain two genders and no theology, and some people would use their God to silence me. That can only increase my stress level to ensure that their God continues to send messages through me. Prophecy is just a stress response. Make someone mad and they will tell you what they really feel.

Sam Sax's novel, *Yr Dead*, published in 2024, is told from the perspective of a queer Jew named Ezra who sets themself on fire and dies. Ezra says that "the myth I love goes like this: In the beginning, there were two people in a garden. They had no genders and had no god."[58]

The phrase "I contain two genders and no theology" has been part of my book, *Bad Fire*, since its first edition in 2019. I'm delighted when two writers independently come up with similar phrases because it means we've alighted on something true.

Invisible and opposing forces are always at work. A bridge is held together by tension and compression and is built full of holes so the wind doesn't knock it over. It has to fight against itself a little. It has to sway. It has to be in the world. It exists to serve a broader context.

More pages would unglue your attention faster. The story holds together by its holes.

Let us say a *bracha*, a blessing: *Blessed art thou, Muse of Books, for the butterfly release into the expanse of what doesn't need to be said.*

In one of my earliest memories — perhaps I am two years old — I am playing with a baby toy. Two spoons are attached at their handles, doubling their length: one end is a spoon facing up, the other is a spoon facing down. I flip it over and over, trying to understand. Why does it always look the same: one spoon convex, one spoon concave? Why can't I line them up differently? Did I flip it 180 degrees or 360 degrees? Does it have one side, two sides, three sides, an infinite number of sides? If I keep peeking around the back (as fast as possible, so the spoon doesn't catch me looking), am I ever going to see anything different?

A more adult way of putting this: The front and back contain and create each other. You don't get one without the other. It's two sides of the same object.

If you want me scraping your database and creating detailed technical documents in your office, you have to accept that I sometimes have difficulty making eye contact. If I am excellent with the machines, I might be less excellent with the people. Yes, I can try to improve multiple skills and learn something new. No, I can't pursue infinite growth in two areas that are in a certain tension with each other. One is the front and one is the back.

Keep flipping a spoon until you convince yourself of this. You'll always see a convexity or a concavity. You can only see one side at a time, so you quickly forget that the front and the back are parts of the same object. Try to remember. Flipping it over one more time is not going to get you to the bottom of it. In principle, the spoon cannot be everywhere convex nor everywhere concave. You can get mad at it, stomp it, and flatten it, but you might be even more disappointed with that outcome because then it's not a spoon at all.

The boss says: "Everyone likes the part of your spoon that holds the soup. But what's with this bumpy part that everyone hates? It's holding you back. You could be a vice president by now if you could hold the soup from both sides of your spoon." This is something a three-year-old would say. This is not good life advice. This is not "actionable."

Looking for bugs in an unfinished software product requires a "front" skill for anticipating errors that must never be allowed to affect the customer. It's imagination. It's attention. It's care. The "back" side effect is that I devote time to "what if?" inquiries about stuff that doesn't exist, won't exist, and just isn't my business. It's pretty much the same thing. I'm the same person. It's a single trait, double-sided. The way you phrase it depends whether you're looking at my face or my ass.

I sit in your car that's sinking into the swamp and spin the wheels until your vehicle jumps onto dry ground. You're mad you heard the wheels spinning. That was the sound of the epic save. I'm doing quite a lot, and you're mad at me because I'm followed by my own shadow?

Some people object to the terms *mental illness* and *insanity* because these terms contain prejudice and wrong assumptions and describe dysfunction and destruction. These people may instead prefer "madness" which has been occasionally more positively used to describe creativity. In a mythological context, too, Patrick Harpur identified *insanity* as outright wrecking-ball behavior and distinguished it from *madness* which grants the "double-vision" in which "one remains oneself while being another."[59]

"All I want to be is a minor augury," says Sam Sax's character Ezra, "the oracle at Delphi huffing fumes off the bituminous limestone." Ezra also says: "I choose gasoline on purpose. It's significant that it'll be a fossil fuel which returns me to dirt: what will end us all and what all this will become in another fifty million years."[60]

People often take pride in their sense of their own difference, and it is of course their right to describe their own experiences and request their own labels. I have my own experience. I see both sides of the spoon. When my brain wasn't working, I felt that was an illness. Anything thicker than water lodged in my throat. I felt my body fat melt away at an alarming rate and I did not know if or when it would stop. A gear, or ten, had slipped. To look back and refer to that period as a state of mystic prophecy seems too sentimental.

Yes, I produced weird art that contained a staggering amount of weird insights, and I retain that skill as a permanent gift. Even today, sometimes the insights come faster than I'd like, as if I'm paging through a cartoon flip book, and I struggle to cram the results in my short-term memory.

But I believe this creativity was a side effect of overactivity and misfirings in my brain. Primarily, it felt *bad*. My temporary feeling of illness in my brain was more akin to what I imagine people feel when a major organ, like lungs or liver, shuts down. The felt imperative was not that I was "different" and that I should accept myself as I was, nor that I was a fount of majestic art; there was, rather, alarm that something was terribly wrong in my body and that I might die. Daily survival was the primary motive, and identification as a mad artist was a secondary amusement. To me, it seems accurate and possibly helpful to pathologize this. Disease, if anything can be called disease, is whatever feels bad or shortens our lives.

Where I do prefer the word *different* instead of *sick* or *wrong* regards my approach to dealing with my own problem. Even though illness itself is not a moral failing, how we respond to illness may reflect upon our character. If someone had noticed my illness and forced a more aggressive treatment upon me, I would have been secretly relieved, appreciative that they tried, and thankful if it worked. But no one intervened. So it was up to me. I exercised. I tried a bad pill. I tried a good pill. I was patient. I made art. Someone might call this approach disordered, dim-witted, or dangerous, but no one else could have solved my nervous breakdown for me. My approach was the only one I could manage, and it eventually worked out.

This isn't a morality tale about "overcoming" illness by force of will, nor is it a miracle tale about winning the lottery. We shouldn't believe we need to do something to "earn" or "deserve" good health, and yet our health comes from somewhere and means something to us. We *are* our brains and bodies; we *are* our health or lack thereof; we're defined by it; our status can change, and the meanings can change. Health, to me, feels more like an organic unfolding. It is a self-discovery.

As an atheist and not a supernaturalist, I believe there are material causes of nervous breakdowns. Something happens in the gray matter or in the intestines. If you're sick, there might be a pill that makes it worse and a pill that makes it better. Your doctor may not be able to tell you which pill is which. A medical solution is a gamble, but it may be a wiser bet than trying to ruminate out of your brain. Medicine might at least treat a symptom or two.

I learned a few facts about bodies which seem to explain what happened to me.

First, the hormones adrenaline and cortisol work in concert. They control how the body experiences and responds to stress. This system is affected by sleep, hydration, and exercise, and it can speed metabolism. The neurotransmitter serotonin plays a role here. I'm guessing this is the system that was apocalyptically disregulated. My engine couldn't jumpstart and jumped in place. That's why I was drinking so much water. That's why the trazodone pill for my serotonin was useful. It took a year of gradual improvement before I had enough perspective even to read about the biological fact that this system exists and consider that something in it had probably snapped. I had to start getting better before I could recognize that I was on the right path.

People who watch horror films experience adrenaline rushes that increase their metabolism. This conclusion was reached several years ago through a study that was not scientifically peer-reviewed and was funded by a video subscription service;[61] regardless, I'm up for using horror movies as an index for metabolic rate. To speed communication about mental health emergencies, people could rank their suffering against the distress they feel watching famous slasher films. I calculate that — based on the calorie-burning numbers reported in the study, my food intake, and my weight loss — during my most distressed period, my metabolism was substantially higher than that of someone watching "The Exorcist" round the clock for two months. A movie in this adrenaline bracket has probably not hit the mass market, but I know what all the scenes look like.

This was the level of stress from which I ran. Though I couldn't outrun my problems, running is a good method of stress management.

Endurance runners have high metabolisms even when they are resting, and this explains why my unintentional weight loss was maintained even when I tried to rest. This explanation is fine.

A few years later, I wrote:

I still don't plan my runs. I don't say "I try to fit exercise into my day." I don't think I will ever say that. It suggests that my mind-body is a small dog and that I make a calm, socially comprehensible decision about when to walk it. Instead, now, I am aware that my mind-body is hitched up to marionette strings that some hurricane-force power will pull when and if it wishes. It probably won't feel out of control as long as I'm calm, happy, and healthy. But, in principle, it could happen again, so it is a force I respect. "I exercise," I say, because that is a fact. I may be exercising a lot or a little, but I don't pretend to be in control of the details, because the details on any given day are a gift that I am given as part of the short time I am alive on earth. I exercise alone.

"Burn your fire for no witness," wrote singer-songwriter Angel Olsen, "it's the only way it's done."[62]

the psychological concept of "dissociation" can (in its broadest sense) apply to how feelings are compartmentalized, and it can intensify after emotional trauma. Maybe a psychologist would tell me I'd been dissociating. I'm not sure if that classification can usefully compare me to anyone else, if dissociation is a culturally constructed experience, if there's a way to argue myself out of it, or what I would otherwise do with that information, then or now.

I don't stick with medical or psychological explanations very long. I wax abstract. *Jouissance* in poststructuralist philosophy is death-driving, soul-smashing emotion so intense that, in the words of Steven Church in *One With the Tiger*, it presents "an opportunity to reassemble oneself."[63] That, to me, makes as much sense as talking about hormones and trauma. So, too, does *duende,* the focus on mortality, both mystical and emotive, that lets us see our lives with such painful clarity that it opens the door to artistic creation and performance. Federico García Lorca said: *"Para buscar al duende no hay mapa ni ejercicio. Solo se sabe que quema la sangre..."* ["To seek duende, there's neither map nor exercise. One only knows it burns the blood..."][64] Karl Jaspers said we end up in "limit situations," *Grenzsituationen,* where we sense our own previous limits and the need to push ourselves beyond them.[65] If we go somewhere new, we'll need new words. If our journey isn't physical, our words may not anchor to anything physical. If we need to distance ourselves from danger while we contemplate danger, we can consider it as an art object; this mood is called the *sublime*.[66]

We can use metaphor well. Metaphor goes bad when we forget how it works and what it is supposed to do. It rots when we begin to take it literally.

If we talk about the mystery of life, for example, a metaphoric frame of mind hums this tune: *No one knows what the world is or how it got here! The only adequate response is to live an ethical life. If you cannot accomplish good, at least be pure of heart.* A creation myth speaks in concrete images, yet those images are asking, *Wow, what's this?*

To a more literal frame of mind, the same creation myth degrades. Now it sounds like: *The planet was created in six days by an invisible man who wants men to throw rocks at women, queers, and pagans.* That literalization means the metaphor has been forgotten, and thus the metaphor is spoiled. The spoilage of the metaphor correlates with the spoilage of lives. When we encounter a metaphor, we need to comprehend it well, and we need to live and let live.

A "Just add facts!" special preparation doesn't enhance a metaphor's truth; it wrecks the metaphor. The metaphor doesn't want to associate closely with too many facts, and it certainly doesn't aspire to become a fact. Fact-flowers grow up the trellis, but the trellis is not the true measure of beauty and goodness, and the metaphor doesn't want to climb that corporate ladder.

What is a fact, anyway? Perhaps this is a straightforward example: *Your height.* But no, maybe not even that. We ask about "height" as if it were a scientific fact with no room for interpretation. But the concept of "height" assumes you can stand with both feet flat on the ground, neither tiptoed nor bent-kneed. Not everyone can stand like this, or stand at all. If your left leg is shorter than your right (as mine was in childhood), then when you stand barefoot, either your left foot is on tiptoe or your right knee is bent, and how should a scientist record your height? If your legs are different lengths, you don't have a height, or you have two heights, or you can change your height depending on the situation. It seems to be some version of a physicist's paradox because your height is one thing spread across two locations (your left and right legs), and you have to stop moving your legs to record your height, and people dispute which freeze-frame is "most accurate," but there may not be a correct answer since your height doesn't exist until you pick a freeze-frame. The person who observes you creates your height. It is a fiction.

Other people won't notice, understand, or absorb this reality, and you'll learn not to explain it to them because it makes them upset.

This also describes being trans.

Some cis people get upset because transness shows gender to be a fiction. It's a mirror that shows *their* gender as a fiction. Trans people like me don't even have to say anything aloud. If a cis person knows what "trans" means, they will draw conclusions themselves.

Sometimes they blame the conclusions on trans people. But the trans is also inside them, at least as a possible future — just as I once had a life that seemed cis before it occurred to me that trans was a possibility, so the cis-and-trans will always be inside me too.

Metaphors aware of their own power are often more useful than non-facts we treat as facts.

The Talmud records an argument about Moses's height. Rabbis argued about some indirect "ten cubits" reference in Exodus. Let's not. Moses didn't exist, cubits aren't a standardized unit of measurement, ten cubits is probably a giraffe's height, and you don't need to look this up in the Talmud, so let's experiment with not having a footnote here. Let's think for one moment about what footnotes aspire to do. Do they try to pin non-facts to facts? How does that work? How often do footnotes cite sources that are factless? Does a footnote ever justify anything? How does your life change when it has one fewer footnote in it?

A seeker approaches the transsexual oracle asking for The Wisdom but demands that The Wisdom be expressed while the seeker stands on one foot. The transsexual oracle says: *Look at you! You don't have a height. You're standing on one foot, so the measurement will be invalid. You're not playing by your own rules. Drop your other foot. There, that's better. Balanced. Unskewed. I can more reliably approximate your height now, but there's still no such thing as height. This teaching has no footnote. There is no fact of the matter. You have always had the power in your ruby slippers if you had only been willing to balance yourself in them. How did you expect to click your heels when one foot was up in the air? Here, take this useless measuring stick.*

Let everyone stop asking "whether transgender people can exist," said the journalist Lewis Raven Wallace, since clearly "we can and do." Let everyone give up trying "to prove the objective realness of trans experience." No one can feel exactly what someone else feels, but that doesn't justify skepticism of what others say about themselves. We don't need to brag that we are unable to know someone else. Let us not appeal to our own ignorance to justify remaining ignorant. Let us stop discrediting others.

Let us instead discuss why we value subjective experiences. We already know that we value our own. And let us instead ask, as Wallace says, "*how* we will exist."[67]

Arthur Frank said something similar about illness. Especially for people who have already been ill, illness is not only a given, it's a known. One might begin an important question by asking: "If I become ill again, or when I do…" And so, "from the ill person's perspective," he wrote, "the central problem is how to avoid living a life that is diminished, whether by the disease itself or by others' responses to it."[68]

How to exist. How to avoid living a diminished life. That's not new. That's been a central question of philosophy since Socrates. *How should one live?*

But they killed Socrates, didn't they, having charged him with atheism and corruption of the youth, because his philosophical question annoyed them. They sentenced him to death and thus they made him kill himself.

My atheism is a position regarding the danger of unsubstantiated beliefs: beliefs that are "woo," to use the affectionate term. We ought to avoid them, but I accept that some woo will always be with us. A lot of woo comes out of misunderstood and misapplied metaphors.

Many metaphors are good and useful until they're applied too literally. That's the difference between a good fire and a bad one. I'm an atheist full of bad fire. I physically see change as if it were on fire. Right here, I'm owning my woo.

Unfortunately, I have no definition for where a symbol ends and an embodiment begins. That's probably why I ended up changing my sex.

I guess I don't need to know what bit me in my mid-30s, as long as it doesn't happen to me again. Maybe I just need to stay away from whatever sets off my unconscious: watch fewer horror movies, hear less violent news, remember less Bible. Or participate in fewer Grave Incidents about which I feel remorse. I'd like others to find the information they need about their illnesses if something similar happens to them, and maybe my story will be in some measure useful.

Sic transit gloria mundi is a Latin phrase meaning "Thus worldly glory passes away." It was used in Roman papal coronation ceremonies for five hundred years. A ritual participant carries a smoldering torch and shouts *"Sic transit gloria mundi"* to remind the gathered crowd that, though the new pope might look like an emperor, someday this one's glory, too, will pass away.

not every illness leads to recovery.

In S. An-sky's play *The Dybbuk,* which he wrote in Russian and translated to Yiddish himself, two new fathers promise to betroth their infants. The boy's father dies shortly thereafter and the girl's father forgets the promise. When the children grow, they do want to marry each other, but the young woman's father betroths her to someone else. The frustrated young man, clutching the kabbalistic *Book of Raziel,* dies in religious ecstasy as the pronunciation of God's name is revealed to him. His spirit (the *dybbuk*) possesses the bereaved young woman, who soon also dies. In this play, there are no resurrections. Resurrection may not even be possible in this metaphysical system. Just because there is *dybbuk*-possession doesn't mean people can conquer death. Here, the dead man can possess another living body but can't repossess his own. So we may have to let go of that expectation.

The Phoenix is a mythical sun-bird that combusts and resurrects from its own ashes. The Phoenix as a surprise is awesome. However, "the Phoenix as an expectation," Arthur Frank says, "becomes a burden, not a liberation."[69] We may be unable to live up to that standard. Just imagine what will happen if the boss hears that your coworker has Phoenixed; now how will you grade yourself from One to Five on your next self-evaluation?

When a music industry executive told the Jewish singer-songwriter Debbie Friedman that she was famous only as "a big fish in a small pond," Friedman replied, "I'm not a fish."[70] This quip reminds me that if we don't like someone else's metaphor (especially one that is used to diminish us), we can simply reject it.

I think of two bad metaphors that I have often heard used against queer people. They're both references to a supposed "slippery slope." In this image, we're all standing on a hot-buttered ski path, where, if one existing social rule is relaxed or rejected, there will be no basis for having any rules at all and we'll find ourselves at the bottom of the mountain in six seconds flat. "Slippery slope problems" are often posed as good-faith questions in search of logical and literal truth, but they're usually just bad-faith metaphors. One, common in the 1990s and 2000s while same-sex marriage was debated, was: *We can't let people of the same gender marry each other because then we'll also have to let people marry dogs.* (This argument became obsolete after years of same-sex legal marriages and nary a dog.) Another was about gender identity, and it is still common today: *We can't let people assert their own genders because next thing you know they'll tell us they identify as dogs.* (This argument *ought* to be obsolete since people do assert our own genders. Unfortunately, the bad-faith arguers flatter themselves by imagining that they have never yet permitted anyone to do so.)

Sometimes the angry skeptics believe their "slippery slope" concern is literal. It's not. It doesn't even make sense that way. It's a metaphor. They mean to say: *your relationship is nonsense, your identity is nonsense.*

The metaphor is wrong. *The metaphor itself is nonsense.* Which means the correct reply is simple.

"What if you thought you were a cat?" one of Jennifer Finney Boylan's friends challenged her when she had just come out in her forties as a transgender woman. Ultimately, she said, she could only shrug: "Well, I'm not a cat."[71]

That's a fine answer. In addition, if one were in the mood, the question could be flipped back at the questioner. Here's an example.

Many Jews still have not comprehended that women are ordained as rabbis. Women have been ordained in increasing numbers over the past half-century, so, while that may be "new" within a long historical timescale, we who are alive today should be accustomed to it. There is not a slippery slope toward "just anyone" being a rabbi; it is still the case that *rabbis are rabbis.* Therefore, when someone with the online handle "Pam" challenged Rabbi Danya

Ruttenberg, *apropos* of nothing, "How are you a Rabbi?," the rabbi responded: "I'm fine a rabbi! How are you a Pam?"⁷²

ariel is the name of the Little Mermaid in the animated film I saw in a theater when I was nine. Characters in the film pronounce her name two ways.

I liked to imagine it was correct to use the "ah" from the original Hebrew: Ah-riel. The name means "lion of God." In just one spot in the Bible (Isaiah 29:1), God uses that name to address Jerusalem. Ah-riel is also a name for

> the 'altar hearth' on which things are slaughtered and burned (as in Ezekiel 43:16). God continues, 'I will cause distress to Ariel; there will be mourning and lamentation, and the city will be like an *ariel* to me,' like an altar where blood is spilled (Isaiah 29:2).⁷³

Now I realize Eh-riel was the intended pronunciation of the movie mermaid's name, to rhyme with that of her boyfriend, Eric. The riddle is in the pronunciation. She wants *air*.

seven years before my husband and I knew of each other's existence, we separately prepared our lives to receive each other.

In 2009, he chose *El día de la independencia de Colombia* to leave his father's house in Barranquilla and fly hundreds of miles to make a new life in Bogotá.

I had also purchased a plane ticket for that day. I did not know it was Colombia's Independence Day. A court in Boston had assigned me that day to sign divorce papers, so I'd paid for my ex to fly in, come to court, and fly far away again at the end of the day. ("Ex" is not only a prefix, but a full word? Then "trans" is also a full word.) This was a step toward me, too, one day making a new life in Bogotá.

Less than two months before my husband moved from Barranquilla to Bogotá and I went to court to divorce my ex, I had found my way down a mountain using the Pythagorean Theorem. Have I told you that story?

While my fantasy league of demons wound down its internecine period, my illness abated and I began to reemerge.

In May 2016, two important events happened simultaneously.

One I was unaware of: In Colombia, an elderly judge died. His home passed to his daughter.

The other I did know: I took my last trazodone pill.

And immediately, the man I would marry came into my life. I knew him clearly when I found him online.

On the surface of the Earth, we were long-distance. I flew to Colombia to meet him. He took me to a butterfly garden.

Butterfly at the conservation park Recinto del Pensamiento in Manizales, Colombia, photographed on my first trip to meet my husband, September 20, 2016.

He was patient with me while I reorganized my life.

I began to recover in a mostly linear upward swing.

M oses walked up Mount Sinai, and God gave him two stone tablets, each inscribed on both sides by God's own hand, front and back. Moses found his way down the mountain again and saw that the people, who had been bored waiting for him, had already begun to misbehave. They had declared a new spiritual leader in his absence. All they could think of was a cow, but they didn't have a cow, so they made a fake one.

"You need to learn to say *dayenu*," Moses said. "Say 'that's sufficient.' Say: 'It would have been enough.'"

Then Moses smashed the tablets because he decided the people didn't deserve them, and God told Moses he'd have to do it all over again, and Moses fasted for forty days, and God gave new tablets to Moses, and Moses' face glowed with an aura.

According to tradition, Moses here received not just the Ten Commandments but the entire Torah. The Torah covers the story from the creation of the world to Moses' death. So if Moses had bothered to read it, he would have known his own future.

He had already lived through the incident in which the people were thirsty and God told him to strike a rock to produce water (Exodus 17). But he had not yet lived through the repetition of this incident (Numbers 20) in which God would tell him he was not doing enough to promote theism and thus would not be allowed to enter the promised land, the Real Place, at the end of the journey.

Depending whether you see the rock-strikings as two similar events occurring in Moses's life or a storytelling duplication of a single event, the Torah's storytelling may not be linear.

Depending whether you believe that Moses received a book with information about things that hadn't yet happened, time itself may not be linear.

Linear improvement was briefly interrupted when, one day, after spending hours scrutinizing a book of mythological interpretation, my throat sealed shut and refused to take in scrambled eggs, shredded potatoes, and water. (The book was Patrick Harpur's *The Philosopher's Secret Fire*.) I was frustrated with my sudden backslide and was cautiously aware, in that moment, that each person has a last meal and that I may have been feeling what it is to stop eating.

I consulted an otolaryngologist who immediately twilighted me and dropped a camera down my throat.

Slowly. Remember how once, when you were small, you "wouldn't / shut the fridge door" too quickly, the poet JK Anowe recalls, and you peered into the fridge because you wanted "to see the inner light go off"? The darkness and the light almost, but not quite, identical with the closing and the opening? You might see it happen if you wait and let it happen. "That's how you tend," Anowe says, "to the heart."[74]

I suppose the doctor saw my fridge light was working because he told me I was going to live. My throat only looked singed, probably from acid reflux. I hadn't considered the possibility. There's a pill for that, too.

Acid reflux, I'd always assumed, affected "old people" — people older than I, according to the mobile threshold of the young/old binary, which it turns out is not a medically valid distinction.

And while *acid* suggests to me the sensation of burning, I learned that acid reflux doesn't necessarily hurt. It can cause trouble swallowing. Food feels stuck in the throat. Food might even get a little stuck for real and come back up because the throat is just not cooperating. Even without trying to swallow, acid reflux can create the illusion of suffocation. It can be related to anxiety and panic. When someone doesn't understand what they're feeling in their body, their panic might rise, ratcheting up the symptoms.

Drowning doesn't look like yelling and waving. Drop the camera down the well: It might look more like an excess of stomach acid.

Let me tell you what feels like a slice of heaven: over-the-counter chewable calcium antacid tablets.

Also, an ice cube to anesthetize the throat.

Or a gelato milkshake. That's why I had liked them so much, though I didn't understand it at the time. Gelato cooled my throat. Plus, gelato has a lower fat content than ice cream, so gelato contributes less to the acid volcano in the stomach than an ordinary milkshake would. Gelato delivered calories when I couldn't swallow anything else.

Additional kindnesses: Less coffee. Less chocolate.

I like staring into databases, but I may have to give those up.

More gazing into butterfly gardens.

I know something about butterflies that is both scientific and abstract. The metamorphosis involves melting down and reforming the caterpillar's insides while keeping it alive. Every internal organ turns into something new, except for its breathing tubes (which are like its lungs), and even those will move around inside its body and reanchor themselves to new structures. Yet the resulting butterfly remains the same animal. It keeps its memories. If you cause physical pain to a caterpillar so that it learns to avoid a particular trap, then, after it becomes a butterfly, it will still avoid that same trap.[75] The events that caused it pain belong to it forever. Those memories are the insect's trauma. The caterpillar becomes a dream inside the cocoon. It will change its entire body but never its history. That creeping green thing can't unfeel and unknow its truths even on the day it spreads purple wings.

"Almost seventy years and nothing has killed me," Ellen Bass writes in her 2017 poem "Indigo." In this poem, she tells her daughter she fears losing her mind and would hope to be euthanized in such a scenario, and her daughter asks, "when's the cutoff?"[76]

through my ruminations on the Grave Incident, I scribbled a couple hundred thousand words about why the Other Transsexual wasn't talking to me, how much I wanted this to change, and so on. I'd need computer data tools to thoroughly map that philosophical account.

Fortunately, there's a sword that cuts through it. The true sword glows, and then you know. After several years and reams of paper, the explanation is:

𝕳𝖊 𝖎𝖘𝖓'𝖙 𝖙𝖆𝖑𝖐𝖎𝖓𝖌 𝖙𝖔 𝖒𝖊 𝖇𝖊𝖈𝖆𝖚𝖘𝖊 𝖍𝖊 𝖉𝖔𝖊𝖘𝖓'𝖙 𝖜𝖆𝖓𝖙 𝖙𝖔.

Everything else is commentary.

back when the Other Transsexual was still talking to me, we often invoked a little cartoon character he invented. The character had a four-letter name, didn't speak but sang a wordless tune, and represented joy and simplicity.

I don't remember if he told me how he came up with its name. As with everything involving this character, the point was not to overthink it.

Nine years after he stopped talking to me, I noticed the meaning of the name isn't in the spelling but in the pronunciation. The character's name sounds the same as the Spanish verb *to swallow*. It sounds the same as the German verb *to take it with you*.

The joy is not in the little drawing. The joy is in you.

running demonically was hard on my feet. Here's how I found out.

In March 2020, my husband and I were quarantined in our Bogotá apartment.

In late April, we were finally allowed out for brief morning exercise — perhaps it was May when I heard the rule had changed. I didn't bother to stretch my legs first. I went out in the early morning and sprinted for a few minutes. I was fine all day.

Then, in the middle of the night, I began to get out of bed and put my feet on the floor in a normal way. My Achilles tendons, both of them, instantly turned to 12-inch steak knives.

As we were quarantined and trying not to catch or spread a virus, I did not go to a doctor's office. I believed letting the injury go unexamined was the lesser of two health risks. I crawled back in bed.

I stayed very quiet. There was a pandemic. People were suffering. No one needed to hear that my feet hurt.

"When I emerge, what will I remember?" Elaine Wang asks in her poem about the caterpillar.[77]

Maybe we won't look back and all we'll have is the desire to move on. *Zugunruhe*, the itch to migrate.

In 2023, each foot has a bone spur at the back of the heel where the Achilles tendon inserts. The tendon is too short to stretch over the spur comfortably. It has tendonosis and is calcifying.

The lateral tendon wraps too loosely around the outside of each foot and doesn't hold the foot together. There, tendosinovitis.

There's another tiny bone spur on the bottom of each foot poking into the sole's soft tissue. Plantar fasciitis is irritation of the tissue there.

The bursa in the heel leaked fluid into the tissue. That's bursitis.

I lost ankle dorsiflexion, meaning that, when I'm standing, although I can flex my toes, I can't further lift the sole of my foot to point toward the sky.

The inside of each ankle lost cartilage, which means another kind of arthritis is starting there. There's a gap at the back of the ankle called an exostosis. I couldn't walk well, so the muscle around the ankle on the front of the foot began to atrophy.

Each foot filled with fluid. By the time I got an MRI, the machine couldn't see through my foot all. The swollen tissue started to crush the bones in my midfoot, as if my foot itself were a tight shoe I couldn't loosen, so I developed midfoot arthritis.

After living with this for three years, I received steroid injections in the tendons, which helped. Some range of motion returned. Most of the time my feet feel as though there's a band pulled tightly around my ankles that's cutting off circulation.

I'm supposed to not let it get any worse.

I mention my feet to illustrate how hard I ran in 2015, how my feet suddenly gave out in 2020, and how I'm still dealing with this as we head into 2025. I'm warning you where your feet may be in five years if you don't run with care today.

I mention my feet to help explain why the word *biological* is a poor synonym for *not trans*. Yes, I'm a trans man, but I'm also a biological man, or else how to explain what's happened to my feet? Do I have non-biological foot injuries? I need doctors to take my biological human status seriously; it's hard enough to get healthcare during a pandemic without having been previously marked as non-biological. When trans people are relentlessly informed we're not biological, it's an obstacle to our belief that we deserve healthcare and can access it. We internalize it. This word *biological* works on a subconscious level and can affect on trans people's physical health.

In conclusion, cis people could please call themselves *cis* instead of *biological*. It would be more accurate and more helpful.

Someone will argue that I'm only one person and that I haven't adequately made my point. That's a way of saying they don't care about what I said. Understood.

My feet will die on this hill.

When my foot pain has been bad, sleeping has been difficult.

Walking has been difficult, depending on the day. Sometimes walking feels fine in the moment but causes a flare-up later.

Stairs feel very bad, especially going down.

I can't run. So I don't.

BAD FIRE

Indigo leaves yield blue dye when they are mixed with ashes and salt water. In Minna Salami's retelling of a legend from the Foya Kamara in West Africa, a goddess petitioned the spirits to grant her the secret of blue dye, then coated herself with ashes from the sacred fire. The spirits took her baby, leaving only indigo leaves in its place, and she wept. Her tears were the final ingredient for the chemical reaction. This legend explains why, as Salami says, "blue is a feminine color in Africa."[78]

We are left with ashes, but any number of marvels might come from ashes.

A legend about the Baal Shem Tov, the 18th-century Polish rabbi who founded Hasidism: He was accustomed to visit a special place in the woods, light a fire, and pray. This ritual assured his success in any endeavor he faced. The next generation omitted the fire, yet the ritual continued to succeed. A generation after that, the prayers were forgotten, yet the ritual continued to succeed. The next generation forgot even the location in the woods. There was no more ritual, yet merely retelling the story of the Baal Shem Tov's mystical powers assured their success in any endeavor.[79]

I no longer have the forest, the prayers, or the fire. But I have this story, and that suffices for the magic.

In 2015, I ingested three weeks' worth of clonazepam pills. I still have the fourth week remaining in the bottle. After someone puts a genie back in a bottle, it doesn't matter whether they throw the bottle into the ocean or keep it. The magic has already been sufficient. *Dayenu*.

Once I used the Pythagorean Theorem to find my way down a mountain. Have I told you this story?

I was hiking a famously steep mountain in Colorado. The mountain's base sits at about 8,600 feet — the same elevation as Bogotá, as it happens — and it rises another 5,500 feet from there. For the first hour hiking up, I shared the trail with joggers and dogwalkers. For the next mile, it was just me.

I began to wonder exactly how steep the mountain was. Could I calculate it? How? *The Pythagorean Theorem*, I thought. Mountains are triangles, and the Pythagorean Theorem was the only triangle equation I remembered. With a stick, I sketched variables in the dirt. But I couldn't reach an answer, and I supposed my question needed trigonometry instead.

I moved on. I hallucinated soap bubbles floating by. The trees chirped *tilíntilín*. I began to chat with myself aloud. I guessed the party in my head was due to a lack of oxygen. I saw signs saying *Beware of mountain lions*. The lions would come for me now. It was time to turn back.

Descending the mountain, the path forked. I couldn't

remember from which way I had come. I chose the left path, but I didn't recognize a single tree. Just when I was about to give up and wander off in my confused state, I observed a disturbance in the dirt: The Pythagorean Theorem! I had sketched it there myself with a stick.

The magical aid is made of symbols, and it will be more helpful if it is physical too.

You are allowed to have a magical gender. You are allowed to change your body too.

Binary sounds to me like advanced math, and *nonbinary* sounds like whatever I didn't study after trigonometry.

If a trans person is a butterfly with antennae forking out, each bobbing its little black ball at the end, maybe the antennae are binary — except that they work together. Anyway, the butterfly is more than its antennae, and I don't know where any binary butterflies are. *Nonbinary* sounds like a mysterious post-butterfly status. To me it's beautiful from the outside, though I don't know what it feels like to inhabit that advanced stage of the life cycle. I can't count the antennae. I can't say *nonbinary* describes me. I can barely handle regular butterfly.

That's an indirect explanation of *what makes a memoir trans.*

More directly: Now you are deep into this memoir, and it is making you trans.

two years after my initial crisis, I left my job calmly and voluntarily, though I don't want to wear that detail as a badge of superiority, as the material outcome to me would have been the same if I had been, so to speak, fired.

I moved on with life. That's the definition of progress. This is a solution.

If I were allergic to carrots, I wouldn't eat carrots. If I had a stick, I wouldn't hit myself with it. Superman is magic, but he doesn't wear the spandex all day and all night and he doesn't have to wear it upon command.

I wrote stories and poems in my office notebook. My handwriting was bad, but time will tell if my ideas were good.

"*Every wish / will find its symbol*, the woman thinks" — that's Rita Dove's conclusion to her poem "History."

After a while, everyone in the story dies: Aaron, Moses, and the world goes on.

After a while, I said: *Maybe the Tabernacle does not have to be maintained anymore. Maybe no one has to do that.*

took a self-declared indefinite hiatus from corporate jobs. That's not an illness; that's the cure. I live differently than other people because I have a different brain. When I take care of my brain, I'm not sick.

The human brain has evolved in a way that allows it to cooperate in modern offices and also to wander off into the snowy woods and see visions. Even if I try again to devote myself primarily to the former, it should not be too surprising if I can still manage the latter. I'm still finding ways to make my little altar sacrifices without setting my tunic on fire. God might speak from a burning bush, but now I can't imagine wanting so much nearness. There is such a thing as too much nearness to The Thing.

The caterpillar-butterfly is pregnant with itself. You cannot pull it out of the cocoon to interrogate it: "What are you: caterpillar or butterfly?" At that point, it is a little vial of goo. If you break it open to look at it, you won't get an answer. It will have been an intermediate thing, and you will have killed it. It's a Schrödinger's cat-erpillar that will only ever be dead when you observe it. We could chalk up that experiment as another Grave Incident, but we'd really like to have fewer of those. There are mistakes that make us declare "How fascinating!," and then there are sins.

If the trans man is vibrating with a high frequency of magic, he's shaking with trauma. Someone wants his magic crystal vibrations but they don't want his crystal to crack, explode, dissolve, crumble to dust. But this is the front and the back. A majority queers a minority, and none of us get a world in which the queer minority makes electric rainbow art without also being mired in weird challenges and undoable tasks for which there are no acceptable words and which they feel the need to discuss especially when no one wants to hear it. The creativity emerges from having to deal with those unnameable challenges. That's the front and the back. We need to stay in community even when the community is scratching us in the half-healed trauma. The rainbow is refracted light. It's a fracture, a breaking. The light bends. So were gay men called "bent." That total package is what it means to be queer. That's why the word "queer" remains alarming. It tells us that the pretty rainbow flag has a back side where the colors aren't as bright and the knots of the threads are visible and dangling.

"*Lautlos nahte sich das Niegeglaubte.*" *The Never-to-be-Believed approached noiselessly,* Rilke wrote of the unicorn. "*Der Beine elfenbeinernes Gestell / bewegte sich in leichten Gleichgewichten.*" *The ivory frame of the legs moved in gentle equilibrium.* "*Und auf der Tierstirn, auf der stillen, lichten, / stand, wie ein Turm im Mond, das Horn so hell, / und jeder Schritt geschah, es aufzurichten.*" *And on the beast's forehead, on that tranquil and illuminated spot, stood — like a tower in the moon! — the horn so bright, and every forward step served to raise it up.*[80]

The effect of the closet: I probably can't work for an investment company again without somehow experiencing emotional harm. I don't know which investment company allows trans people to bring our full spectrum of the honest everything: the anger when we are hurt, the madness, the what. Someone will argue with me by finding and citing an example of another trans person who has wrangled a "more successful" outcome by investment company standards. That "successful" person, I may counter, was probably born with two balanced hips, yes? I wasn't. Everyone is fighting their own invisible battles. I can't tell you how to balance yourself. I can only show you how I balance myself.

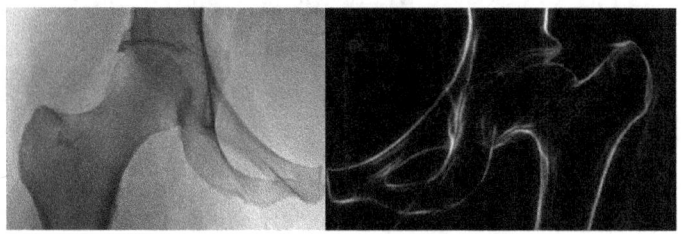

X-ray of my hips, age 32.

We are *being-doings*. Everything is a performance, but the performance is who we are. The existentialist philosophers said something like that. And our operations often aren't conscious. The performance is a half-sleepwalk with specters. Our autopilot, as much as our choices, makes us who we are.

Sometimes others criticize our automatic behavior as if it were not only deliberate but an affront against them. When we don't conform, strangers ask us why we appear so oddly gendered, instead of granting us "the luxury of being," Alok Vaid-Menon writes. In these cases, "I am only seen as doing. As if my gender is something that is being done to them and not something that belongs to me." All of us are always *being-doing* our lives, so the question is why anyone views another's *essence-performance* as a threat. According to the moving goalposts of feminine and masculine, Vaid-Menon says, "we are both too much and never enough." We see what the goalposts are meant to do: not to assess reality nor pursue goodness but to uphold a meritocracy that has standards for the sake of having standards and that judges for the sake of judging. "The gender binary is set up for us to fail. For us all to fail."[81]

The concepts of "success" and "failure" collapse into each other when you stare into them, as do the concepts of man and woman, thinness and fatness, sickness and health, speed and slowness, intent and spontaneity, request and surprise, quehaceres y nadaquehaceres, warp and weft, rupture and reparation, canon and commentary, order and innovation, normal and queer, reality and dream, want and indifference, critic and fan, symbol and babble, signal and noise, beginner and expert, discovery and epiphany, binary and nonbinary, yes and no, come and go, God and No God.

Some traditionally observant Jews pray in a gender-segregated room. The curtain that prevents men and women from seeing each other is called the *mekhitza*.

I've heard from Jews who have tried to honor this tradition while also trying to be egalitarian and inclusive. It has rolled out like this. Each congregant may assert their own gender: man, woman, or something else. There are three prayer spaces: *Man*, *woman*, and *gender-neutral*. Men and women are not permitted in each other's prayer spaces but may go to the gender-neutral space, so they have two spaces available to them and can move between the partitions while praying. Whoever feels gender-fluid or gender-free can move between all three spaces. In practice, the system — as I've been told — breaks down, because the original intent of a stable partition between differently gendered people is no longer in place. The question becomes: Why restrict anyone's movement? And the original question arises anew: Why do Jews gender-partition the prayer space? Could we just not?

Those are fairly concrete issues that spring up when a community is dealing with a tangible *mekhitza*.

Yet more metaphorical issues occur to me.

If you want to see people who are gendered differently from you, and especially to see people who are neither men nor women, you have to tear down part of the *mekhitza*. You may not need to leave your seat, but you at least have to poke holes in the curtain. It's not that nonbinary people are sitting on the "other" side of the aisle from you; it's that the *mekhitza* changes the way we see other people. It's a lens of distortion.

As long as we have a mental *mekhitza* dividing everyone into two camps, we can't sincerely recognize anyone as nonbinary. They might already be sitting next to us, but the existence of the *mekhitza* implies that there are only men and women, and that those who can't conform or who won't fit in are causing conflict.

If, on the other hand, we give up the metaphorical *mekhitza*, then there is no longer any partitioned binary, none of us any longer have a place in it, and we've outgrown communities and systems that are still enacting the *mekhitza* we wrecked. Without capital-G Gender, each of us is fully human, comprehensible, and deserving of equality, regardless of our little-g genders. We can't go back in the cage because we have been transformed by flight.

You have to make "either-or" choices. You are offered a clonazepam pill and a trazodone pill. One binds to your GABA neurotransmitters, and the other stirs up your serotonin. You don't know what either will do until you pick one, swallow it, and wait.

But you aren't binary. You are less binary with every passing moment.

Someday, probably, an office should hire me again. They would get something special. But I do not know yet if I want to give it to them.

That's what I wrote in earlier versions of *Bad Fire*. In this third *Bad Fire*, I am starting to know I do not want to give it to them.

The direwolf will never be a sled dog even if it offers that service. The yoke fits too tight. A metaphor doesn't want to become a fact. It would not be able to breathe. The wind wouldn't find enough holes to pass through the bridge. The bridge would topple.

As long as I'm literalizing my paradise, I'm picky about what I include in it. I may not request to enter the office. I may wait to be asked to dance. The invitation may work for me only if it feels like a surprise.

When Eve and Adam transgressed, God punished them. *You, Eve,* God said, *will give birth in pain. And you, Adam,* God added, *must work to live.* As an abstraction, especially one that must be translated to fit modern concepts, the *must-ness of work* is increasingly fuzzy. Workers today are so alienated from the means of production. If I were starving, I'd know it, and I wouldn't have energy to discuss the meaning of necessity. But if the hunger is not in my stomach, and if I don't feel the necessity of work for my personal survival, then where does that demand come from? What system tells me *must*? Must do *what*?

The idea of work as punishment — as *stick* — doesn't activate me. An actual stick would surely activate me, but an imaginary stick doesn't. Perhaps that's because I don't believe in God and certainly not in a punishing God.

The idea of work as invitation — as something closer to *carrot* — smells better, earthier, rooted. Sometimes there's a *must-ness* in the way we respond to an invitation. When we smell food, when we draw near to the thing, it's less an idea and more a recognition. We recognize the invitation. There is hunger, or joy, or a mirror image of ourselves, and it is irresistible.

Tell us a story in English. I can do that.

Now translate it into Spanish. I can do that.

I might have to work to live. Or to help someone else live. Or to help the world live.

There's the "work" of *tikkun olam,* repairing the world. That's different from "work," the yoke given to Adam to turn paradise into an agricultural field. These types of work may be complementary or oppositional, depending on how you cultivate your field.

When I ask whether I must work to live, the answer depends on who is hungry and what is hungered for. The answer can change with the hunger. I can reassess the need. The lesson can be ongoing.

i am never running against the other runners. The race is always organized by age and gender. The other men are six feet tall and they ran track in high school. I have a lopsided female pelvis. I am in their gender category because at some point in my life I asked for that. I expect to finish the race and I expect to be the slowest man. Maybe no woman will be slower than me either, and I will be the slowest human. It does not matter.

I keep these old words in present tense, even though now I have arthritis and there is no race.

You can run without measuring your pace. Devin Kelly writes about competition and commodification:

> In what ways can we recognize the race we are each running, on our own separate tracks that have no specific shapes, where there is no such thing as time, no such thing as an Olympic record? It is the exactness of time that destroys us. It is the way time has been commodified. It is the how-much-can-you-fit-in.[82]

If that is true of your footprints through the snow in the cemetery at night, can't it also be true of your daytime efforts in the workplace?

In my imagination-memory, I am in the boss's office and he asks me where I want to be in five years. He needs an answer right now. He doesn't need to do anything with this information, but he wants to know that I have my own answer. If I cannot immediately engage a question that the system believes to be important, it will appear I don't share the system's values and the boss will have to treat me as less valid.

What job do I want five years from now? To imagine my best self in my future, I suppose I must first connect with a true self in my past.

I try to remember every job I've ever had. I dredge up memories of jobs I've almost forgotten. I remember that, when I was eight, I liked a parody of Dragnet in which mathematicians solved crimes. One partner was a woman, the other a man. I, too, wanted to be a crime-fighting mathematician. This is a job role you can actually have at an investment company. But now I think it is not possible for me, because I have also seen the film *A Beautiful Mind* in which a mathematics professor hallucinates, and I am pretty sure that if I went for a mathematics degree, I would never learn trigonometry but would start to hear voices. The backside of data analysis would for me present as much larger than the front.

I gaze farther into my past. When I imagine my very beginning, I discover a universal answer about what we humans are supposed to do.

Each human being comes into this world assigned exactly the same entry-level job. (Our requirements soon increase, but never mind them just for now.) When a child is born, as it emerges from its sealed place in the womb water, it has only a few seconds to perform this first job. If the adults don't hear it fulfill its obligation, they'll gather around it and watch its face until it happens. It needs to open its mouth and let the emptiness in.

Its second job is to swallow. The impulse comes from the brainstem, the simplest part of the brain that can operate unconsciously, but swallowing requires the coordination of a couple dozen muscles. The throat splits two ways: the esophagus to the stomach, the trachea to the lungs. It's a kind of binary. It's not always exactly a choice. The child needs to swallow liquid into its stomach and not into its lungs. Then it needs to pause to breathe. *Swallow. Breathe. Swallow. Breathe. Alternate, back-and-forth, all the time.*

The blessing called *Asher Yatzar* acknowledges God for creating humans with

> many openings and many hollow spaces. It is obvious and known before Your Seat of Honor that if even one of them would be opened, or if even one of them would be sealed, it would be impossible to survive and to stand before You even for one hour.

In 2023, my husband and I bought a home in Bogotá, seeking a place within the same city that would be easier on my feet than the apartment we'd rented for six years.

As we signed papers at a table with the former owner, she told us she had inherited the property when her father died.

After we moved into the home that had become our property, we looked up this former owner. He had been a judge who died on about the same day in 2016 that my husband and I noticed each other online and considered whether to contact each other. Two days after the judge's death, I sent a greeting to this man, my future husband. From there, the judge's daughter waited seven years to sell us the home.

A closing that allowed for an opening.

Sugar is appetizing again but only in moderate amounts. Candy no longer helps with sadness, distraction, or anxiety. I still like chocolate occasionally, especially in coffee, but it does not regulate my mood and I have no metabolic craving for it. It tastes like food from an earlier stage of my life. It tastes as if it should not fit into my mouthparts. Chocolate tastes to me now as leaves taste to butterflies. It happened in an instant one day when I was thirty-five, and my brain never returned to the way it was before. This is the force of emotional trauma. It can rewire chemistry.

Zenju Earthlyn Manuel asks what we feel, and who we become, when we gaze at "leftover pieces from things that needed to be destroyed for the sake of well-being—personal and collective." This effort is "not dressing up darkness or making it sweet to swallow. It is not making it presentable or putting language to it so that the world accepts it. It is opening to all that darkness gives and changes, whether desired or not."[83]

Most of me is still here. I am tougher, less afraid.

If you get it, dear reader — if you have reached this point in the book, and if you hear the still, small sound of the change — then the Transsexual Oracle hereby gives you permission to call yourself *trans*.

If you say you're trans, it's a double-edged blade: some people won't believe you, and others will. Be careful what you wish for.

Trans is a flexible beginning for a word. You can pick your own secret suffix. The best suffix for you may not be *-gender* or *-sexual*. Only you know how you want the word to sound. The word *trans* is an abbreviation because we have never known the correct pronunciation of the full word.

We show up, and that's how we learn not to settle for less from ourselves, from others, from systems. "When I think of care, I think first of him," Malatino says of his childhood friend who was also trans, and of their "pattern of care and witness" that "raised the bar for every significant encounter and intimacy to come. This is about a certain kind of faithfulness and a certain kind of obligation: about what we owe each other."[84]

We were married in January 2017. I flew to Bogotá and we went to a public notary.

"*Bashana haba'ah, nifros kapot yadayim mul ha'or hanigar halavan*" ("Next year, we will spread out our hands toward the radiant light") are Ehud Manor's Hebrew lyrics to *Bashana Haba'a*.[85]

I flew back to Boston alone.

In November, I left Boston. I quit my job, sold my condo, and boarded an airplane to live with my husband in Bogotá.[86]

When I got down to the big tasks of my exodus, it only took three weeks for me to stop my old routine and take my seat on that plane. I do not recommend this timeframe for a large move.

Here in Bogotá, when I order a mocha, the cashier asks my name. They intend to write it on the empty coffee cup and pass the labeled cup down the line so another barista can call out my name when my drink is ready. It's the same procedure as in Boston and probably every other place in the world that uses disposable cups, but it plays out differently for me in Bogotá than it did in Boston.

I say my name. The cashier is apprehensive. Never mind that the name once meant "torturer" in Anglophonic lands; the problem in Colombia is that this name is difficult to say and spell. The cashier did not anticipate a foreign customer with a foreign name. We get it written on the cup: "TUCKER," four consonants, one of which is silent, and two unpronounceable vowels from another continent. I don't fear how a stranger interprets this name. I'm happy I'm going to hear something like my name and the mispronunciation will mean my coffee is ready. When it's time to call me, the barista takes a valiant guess: "TO CARE." This interpretation of my name is valid, too. I had to come all the way here to discover this.

"Our life, like the Torah scroll, has no vowels. It is left to each of us," Rabbi Gershon Winkler wrote, "to determine our life pronunciation, our story, our interpretation of every turn of our life cycle."[87]

I can swallow. My left hip can bear my weight. My weight is stable.

Once in Bogotá, I wasn't compelled to exercise every hour — anyway, I couldn't. It was difficult to run during the day due to the street traffic. I wouldn't run at night because it wasn't safe. (My husband tells me something happened to him on the street, not once, but *twice*.) In Boston, I ran in the snow, but in Bogotá, there's no snow in which to run. Finally, I lay on the couch. I could do so for an entire day in my pajamas when I was determined to do so. This was an accomplishment.

When I stopped indulging the breakdown, it went away. It was all headache and no substance. All hat and no cattle. Or, as it is said here, the truck is *puro tilintilín y nada de paleta* — all ding-a-ling and no ice cream.

I indulged other parts of me, other goals. I took better care of myself. Having acid reflux means I have a medical excuse to eat gelato. I ate a little more oatmeal than I expected to require before my fortieth birthday, but that's OK. I can eat a donut, sometimes pronounced "dona" in Bogotá, which reminds me that it is a gift.

The donut is shaped like a throat. It is matter and emptiness. "The center of gravity of a donut is not in the donut. It's in the hole," Dan Barker said in his book on free will.[88]

trying to gather people and experiences, hold them still, and make them yours is like standing over the ocean surface and trying to pull bits of light and shadow and small living fish with your bare hands from the water. There's nothing to be gotten that way. Truths can't be harvested. But the light, the shadow, the fish are real; you can swim in the ocean.

You can touch the world without reference to gender and without reference to God. Spanish-speakers (especially in the United States) who wish to avoid the masculine *Latino* and the feminine *Latina* sometimes use the neutral *Latinx*. The *x* is a consonant that might be a vowel. Those who wish to avoid the masculine *ateo* and feminine *atea* [atheist] can use the neutral *ate@*. The @ is a keyboard symbol that might be a donut. People pronounce these neutral forms as they like. No God smites atheists for pronunciation errors.

Of the "Hermetic vessel" that is "the doughnut-shaped torus," Patrick Harpur wrote in his book on mythology: "The alchemical interchangeability of spirit and matter becomes the interconvertibility of energy and mass." A "miles-long" particle accelerator separates the atomic parts; a torus-shaped fusion reactor brings them back together. Through these efforts, physicists discover "the *metaxy*, the in-between world: between wave and particle, observer and observed, mind and matter. At the furthest limits of matter no less than of mind the intermediate realm of 'subtle bodies' takes on new life."[89]

near the Bogotá apartment where I lived for six years, a large plaza houses several banks. An outdoor escalator takes people to the first floor and, from there, skyscrapers rise twenty stories. Walking the neighborhood, I saw other tech companies in gated buildings. I knew them only from the outside. *Someday*, I thought, *one of these companies might take me in. They might want a quiet transsexual dilettante who has intense feelings, who often gets the right answer, who sometimes makes statements that are answers to no known question.*

The infant Moses performed his first and second jobs correctly — he breathed, he swallowed — and then, born into slavery, he had to do his own next simple job: he had to be quiet. He must not have cried much, because his mother hid him for three months. The baby was "good," the text says (Exodus 2:2). But eventually she had to place him in a floating basket on the river.

As long as we live, we look down that river. There is always a next job, until we can't anymore, or until we redefine what we mean by a next job.

I thought I might want to work at one of those tech companies, again, when it was time.

Then again, I thought, maybe not.

If it isn't time for a long time, I may begin to suspect it will never be time, and at that time I may decide the question will have answered itself.

Have I ever wondered what happens inside those buildings or who works there? Have I ever read a magazine article about those tech companies, looked up their job postings, or tried to wrangle a lunch date?

After a few years, the question answers itself.

As Audre Lorde's body was treated for cancer and she acknowledged her mortality, she wrote: "Who can ever really have power over me again?"[90]

Usually, we don't observe who and what is before us. Or we try to observe, but still, we can't really know who and what we're looking at.

We don't know what people are going through.

We don't know what constraints they are shedding.

"This feat is so invisible," says Ellen Bass in her poem about a midlife shift, a poem I still remember two decades after I first read it. "All you can see" is someone "taking herself to the movies, / reading in bed." Yet now, using "only the primitive knife of need, I cut / and splice the circuitry of my brain. / I change."[91]

The larval transsexual climbs into a cocoon and later emerges as the same transsexual at a more advanced stage in its life cycle. You could stop and take a close look: Its gray hairs are an amazement. Actual gray hairs! This mid-life transition is disappointing only if you expected the young transsexual also to become an investment company vice president. You can adjust your expectations and assumptions. The caterpillar was never meant to become an orca. It is amazing as it is, and amazement does not come in degrees. The butterfly is amazing, *period*.

Some might see this as giving up, but our life choices are as much about what we give up as about what we take in. I think we have to give things up gracefully. We have to let the wind pass through us. It is good to be aware of what food we are taking in before we swallow it. We can let wind and water extinguish the flame.

"We are made and unmade," Devin Kelly writes, "in a world that tells us, every day, a different way to be made and unmade."[92]

From reading psychoanalysis in the 1970s, Peter Chadwick absorbed the advice that his worsening pain would eventually "get better," especially if he continued to process the pain. "But it never did. It just got worse and worse and worse. They lied to me. The bastards."[93] The pain is real, and we don't want to be criticized for it. We each believe ourselves "an unrecognized Job," E. M. Cioran wrote, and we never accept the judgment of "someone who has suffered less than ourselves."[94]

But then what?

What if "five years from now I'm flinging my loneliness onto strangers whose only sin is not appearing to hurt as much as I think I do," Leslie Gray Streeter asks in her memoir on grief — is that an acceptable outcome? "If it doesn't get better, guys, what's the point? There has to be a point, right?"[95]

I do not know if there is a point. No God tells me there is.

"There wasn't a future with a happy ending," Rachel A. Rosen writes in her novel *Cascade*. But surely "there had to be something past the next few months beyond fire and void."[96]

If I'm repeating a useless cycle, I can quit and work on a different problem.

Elyn Saks said she had been taught "an unflinching attitude toward illness or weakness: *Fight it*." But "it is *not* necessarily true that everything can be conquered with willpower. There are forces of nature and circumstance that are beyond our control, let alone our understanding, and to insist on victory in the face of this, to accept nothing less, is just asking for a soul-pummeling. The simple truth is, not every fight can be won."[97] If we are in an unwinnable fight, we can accept defeat, move on, and pick a different fight.

That might be the point.

To live truthfully and bring ourselves to tell the truth, to know ourselves from the inside as well as the outside, is a big project. It's a project to which capitalism does not directly assign value, but it is important work because it is what we need from ourselves and each other.

"A thing," Kati Standefer wrote, "never happens once. A thing happens all the time, is still happening right this instant — to us or to other people. And the thing turns into other things, transmutes, burns up, reappears."[98]

In the Book of Exodus, after Moses saw the burning bush in the wilderness, he made a decision.

In January 2017, he went back to the city, approached Pharaoh, and said, "Let my people go." The reply was: "No." Because of this push-and-pull, everyone saw the river turn to blood.

In February, Moses tried again: "Let my people go." Pharaoh said: "No." The push-and-pull caused everyone to see frogs.

In March, Moses-and-Pharaoh said "Let-my-people-go-please-no-but-thank-you-anyway." They broke out in lice.

In April, Moses said, "I am going to try this again." Pharaoh said, "Why bother?" The air was thick with biting flies.

In May, Moses said, "We are going to have to leave." Pharaoh said, "There are still so many bricks for you to make here." Their cows fell over dead.

In June, Moses warned Pharaoh, "I am making a plan to leave." Pharaoh said, "No you're not." Deeply allergic to what he had just said, his skin erupted in blisters.

In July, Moses said, "Now is a good time to let my people go." Pharaoh said, "But the weather." It hailed.

In August, Moses said, "Have you heard anything I've said?" Pharaoh said, "Not really." The air was overcome with the buzzing of a billion locusts.

In September, Moses said, "I cannot believe I am still here talking to you." Pharaoh said, "You're doing great work." They heard each other but could not see each other in the total darkness.

In October, the firstborn disappeared. Moses said, "This is not really a request. I have been here eleven years since this company was a startup. This dinosaur is no longer having fruitful conversations with the other dinosaurs. And who are all these tiny mammals scurrying about? It is long past my time to go. Your firstborn is headed out the door. Sorry-not-sorry." And he said "Goodnight Moon" to his laptop and his chair and his cubicle, and he left. He did not know exactly what he was going to do with all his free time, but he realized that the knowledge to build a Tabernacle had always been inside him.

midnight. It was midnight when the firstborn disappeared. The Torah portion is called *Bo*, after God's command to Moses; it means "come" and also means "go." Probably Moses had muttered under his breath "a feier zol im trefen" [*a fire should burn him*],⁹⁹ and now look what has happened. Pharaoh, seeing the dead strewn everywhere, tells Moses and Aaron: *Yes, go already! Go. Get out of here.* In the next portion, *BeShalach*, since the Hebrews must keep running day and night to escape, God takes the form of a pillar of fire to lead them through the darkness.

When Moses was held in the arms of his birthmother, he was in the moral injustice of slavery, so he was not in the Real Place. When he was growing up with his adoptive royal family, he was separated from both his origin and his destiny, so he was not in the Real Place. When he spent most of his life crossing the desert, he was not in the Real Place. When the Hebrews reached the promised land, God told Moses to climb the mountain and look out over the land: *Everyone else is allowed to enter the Real Place, but the Real Place is not for you. You will die here looking at it.* It was a Real Place to everyone else but not to Moses insofar as he never set foot in it.

We can never grasp our own authenticity. Even to identify an authentic part, we have to recognize it as an object, and then it's no longer part of us because we've split it off. It has become an object of study and criticism. "I know when something *feels* authentic," said Zander Nethercutt, but the challenge is that "in labeling it as such, I've begun the process of rendering it decidedly not."[100] Only entropy. Authenticity is always decaying. When we reflect on part of ourselves, it becomes a matter of nostalgia; it's the unreflected, invisible parts we might call "authentic," were we thinking about them at all. The past isn't quite as real as the present; it's the newer parts that are more authentic.

Now we see that the emperor has no clothes. If he wore clothes, he wouldn't be the Real emperor. Everything we gild becomes a mere idol. The Real is whatever we can't wrap our silk around. The day we hide it in a silk cocoon is the day it begins to die to what it was and to turn into something else. The Real exists by definition, but from a philosopher's perspective, the Real does not exist and never exists insofar as it can't be grasped. The emperor has no clothes because he isn't yet in human form. When he takes human form and wears the silk, he isn't the Real emperor anymore.

You can't enter the Real Place because you're too atheist, God tells Moses.

I'm sorry I smashed the Ten Commandments, Moses says.

It's not that, God says. *I can always make more commandments. But remember that one day in the desert when you argued with me, you broke faith with me, you did not sanctify me? You didn't publicly thank me for giving you water when you were thirsty! That's going to be a problem for us. I mean, there's atheism, and then there's atheism.*

Oh, says Moses. *I don't suppose it's too late for me to change?*

Your fate is foretold, God says, *and now you can only ever be trans. You will reach the other side of the desert but you will not go in. You are never allowed to stop being trans. Right here on the edge of the mountain, on the edge of the Real, they will bury your very trans bones. You are the change.*

I wonder if the authenticity life-cycle might ever flow in reverse: from less to more authentic. It might happen if the specific quality we're concerned about, the known object, fades away to become a forgotten integral part.

Transsexuals begin our gender transitions by putting our gender under a microscope for professional judgment. We ask professionals to allow us to be transsexuals. This is the hour in which we must insist on the authenticity of our gender feelings but also the hour in which we are least able to be authentically ourselves because we are self-scrutinizing. We can't be fully real when we have to weigh the risk of others withholding their emotional validation and material support.

Many years later, when "transsexual" isn't even a word anymore and when we have forgotten that we ever were transsexuals but somehow we are still living our ancestral transsexual ways, as if in a waking dream, having no words for the obvious and incontrovertible, ceasing to argue about it — only then, perhaps, do we finally become *authentically* transsexual. Perhaps we are trans.

In the Biblical story known as the Binding of Isaac, God tells 99-year-old Abraham to circumcise himself, promising a son to him and his 90-year-old wife Sarah. After some happy years, God tells Abraham, "Go sacrifice your son." No questions asked, Abraham gathers murder tools and sets out on a three-day journey to the murder place. "Where's the sheep?" the boy, Isaac, asks his father. "Leave that to God," Abraham replies. He makes his son carry the firewood up the mountain, then ties him up and lifts the knife.

"Ni!" Abraham shrieks (in my own Monty Python-inspired version of this story). It's a word between "yes" and "no," and it nearly kills you to hear it.

Isaac thinks really hard what he wants. He prays for: A *shrubbery!*

Lo and behold, an angel appears.

First, the angel tells Abraham: "Stop! You passed the loyalty test!"

Then, the angel acknowledges Isaac's prayer, and suddenly there is a shrubbery, and there is a ram caught by its own horns on the branches.

"Oh good," says Abraham, "I can sacrifice the ram instead."

The ram is bewildered, having just been called out of its void like Janet on *The Good Place*, or having come from wherever things hang out before we pray for them to appear: it materializes out of nothing, teleports from somewhere else, retroactively just happens to be on location, or is winked from the stars.

I am thinking about this from the ram's perspective because I am an Aries and the ram is my sign.

The ram has just learned a difficult lesson, but it doesn't know what that lesson is. It is a ram, and it is not given any time to ruminate.

Aries, the ram. The four stars in the constellation are labeled with the Hebrew for God, an angel, Abraham, and Isaac.

The loss that prompted my upset wasn't a fiction. It was real. Accepting the realness of my loss lets me "navigate my fear, sadness, and regret within a comprehensible reality system." From my essay "The Trail of His Flames":

We maintain some privacy without hiding, accept some labels without lying, let go of profound pain without erasing, and learn to 'turn away' and yet 'face things.' That means we deflate imaginary monsters of our own making while accurately recalling what has been done to us and what we have done to others.[101]

In December, Jews celebrate the festival of lights. Having revolted against the Seleucid rulers who ordered them to worship Greek gods, the Jews won and regained control of the Second Temple in Jerusalem. With only one day's worth of lamp oil to illuminate the damaged Temple while it was being restored and rededicated, the candles somehow cast light for eight days. They didn't need quite as many calories as they thought they'd need. The caloric value was miraculously stretched. Today we eat fried food — potato latkes and donuts — to recognize the connection between the fuel and the light.

Natalie Eilbert's poem "Imaginal Discs" ends: "The year of out of order. When will repetition / bore through me. Why. They needed to die in a narrative way."[102]

Five years have passed, and I am still alive.

If I could go back five years, before everything happened, and show my old self this tale I have written, this book I call *Bad Fire*, I wonder what I'd have made of it.

From Russell Hoban's novel *Pilgermann*:

> ...the main theme of the people of Abraham: the furnace and the torch; the consuming fire and the onward flame.

> If you measure with what is called time it's a long way from here back to Abram's pieces. But still there is the division of the animals of us, still the thick darkness, the smoking furnace, the flaming torch. And still there are covenants to be made between the pieces, between one fire and another. I am only the waves and particles of such as I was but I have a covenant with the Lord, the terms of it are simple: everything is required of me, for ever.[103]

In the first chapter of Genesis, God created plants, then animals, then male and female humans. In the second chapter of Genesis, God created a male human, then plants, then animals, then a female human. I do not know why the creation story is doubled and irreconcilable with itself. I do not know why God couldn't just create the world once and leave well enough alone without making the very act of creation pluripotently trans.

In the Book of Leviticus, after an improper sacrifice brings about the death of Aaron's sons Nadav and

Avihu (I call them Team Caterpillar), Moses immediately gives new sacrificial instructions to two of Aaron's surviving sons (I call them Team Butterfly). They are to be the new "sons of Aaron" sacrificial assistants. But again, Aaron's family, not having quite learned their lesson, doesn't follow the ritual instructions to the letter. They burn the sacrificial goat though Moses gave them permission to eat it. The reason — or, better, the emotion — for cremating the goat is that Aaron feels that God would be displeased if he ate sacrificial meat right now. (Consider everything that has happened to the family this morning. Nadav and Avihu's ashes are still warm.) Aaron just doesn't feel like eating. Moses is initially angry, but Aaron explains his sentiment, and Moses gets it. Besides, Aaron is a prophet too, so his intuitions about God carry some weight.

This, according to someone long ago who bothered to count, is the exact midpoint of the Torah: Moses launching an inquiry to micromanage whether Aaron's family handled this particular doomed goat exactly as he had instructed. The Torah has 79,976 Hebrew words. The two words in the center are *darosh darash*, "thoroughly investigated." The exact midpoint is the blank space between the words, between the diligence and the act, between the well-doneness and the doing, the unlettered part of the animal skin on which the story is written. Passed down to us is an analysis of eighty thousand words but the innermost core is not any word at all.[104]

The cud was chewed and the whole animal was incinerated. When you lay out a brick arch, you have to put extra space in the joints near the key brick at the center because that space keeps the whole thing standing up. Not the weight but the lightness.

Right after the *darosh darash* of the goat, God gives the laws of *kashrut*: everything we are and are not allowed to eat. Ruminants with cloven hooves are good. In case it is unclear, the camel, hyrax, rabbit, and pig do not meet these criteria and are impermissible. Fish are fine, but if you pull something from the water and it does not have fins and scales, it's not a fish. Most birds are fine, unless otherwise specified. Flying insects are allowed only if they have jumpy knees like grasshoppers. Don't even think about rodents, lizards, snails.

Those rules sound straightforward, but we were told quite a lot of other Biblical things before we were deemed ready to hear what is healthy and proper to eat. Eating is therefore not so obvious, after all.

The "seriousness" of the acid reflux depends on how "seriously" I take it. That is: If I acknowledge the acid reflux as real and care for myself by eating properly (fewer carbs, less fat), the ailment goes away. But if I ignore it and continue to misunderstand my own body signals, the severity dials up. *A shadow. Another back to my front. An unlit inside to my outside.*

When I'm in the mood for a cold drink, it's often because my throat wants the anesthetic. It is good to listen to this request from my body. It might get me ahead of a problem.

If I suddenly feel like I can't breathe, I can ask myself whether I ate a French fry, and if the answer is yes, I can stop eating French fries, calm down, suck some ice, and prevent my thoughts from spinning out of control.

My throat will loosen.

I am fortunate that this is how it works for me. For me, this time, there is an answer. It used to be hard. Now it is easy.

t rans people learn to tell stories in which our lives begin in unhappiness yet we will be made whole through gender transition, never to suffer again. If we are allowed to transition, no malaise of ours shall ever distress anyone else. This is a story that many people, including trans people, like to hear. It's how we gain access to gender transition. It's how we keep media attention positive. It's how we avoid scrutiny. It's how we hold on to our basic rights to exist, tenuous as they are.

However, simplistic narratives shortchange us as humans. As Awkward-Rich says: "Trans discourse that disavows bad feeling is insufficient to the task of learning how to live with, through, and despite it."[105]

t his is the difference between pain and suffering. Suffering is the halo around any pain you don't accept. Suppose you want to have a baby, be a soldier, change your sex. You have a lot of warning that it's going to hurt. If you choose that path anyway, it's often straightforward to accept the painful parts of the process because the pain is part of your choice. You can frame it as a negotiation and make that compromise explicit, or you can just let it happen and quietly accept what comes, but either way, you know your pain is part of something bigger. Whereas, if you protest and resist each difficulty, you will suffer, and the suffering will just add a layer of unnecessary pain.

Pain is the biological feature. The suffering is the psychological bug.

Socially, we're challenged to acknowledge our real hurts — the pain and the suffering — so that we can choose what injuries to avoid, what injustices to fight, what tradeoffs to accept. We can't wish it all away, but we can work to make some of it go away.

We can also learn to detect the role played by our own minds. If we can learn to sense the real acid distress in our bellies and if we can feed ourselves more carefully, maybe we won't falsely imagine that we are being suffocated.

"When we choose a goal," Mihaly Csikszentmihalyi wrote in *Flow*, "and invest ourselves in it to the limits of our concentration, whatever we do will be enjoyable. And once we have tasted this joy, we will redouble our efforts to taste it again. This is the way the self grows."[106]

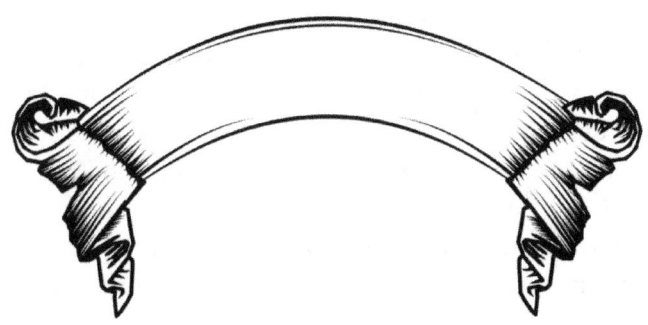

You are trans at this very moment. It may not be obvious: it may neither hurt you nor please you, and it may be deeply unconscious.

You may not be ready. But it happens without your consent. So does your breathing.

If this story has not made you trans, it is only because you already were trans. I do not know what this book will do to already-trans people. I do not think it will set them on hallucinatory fire in the middle of the night; if I had suspected that outcome, I wouldn't have published it. I think something else will happen to already-trans people.

If the idea of being made trans feels like an assault or humiliation, perhaps it is because a hostile system relentlessly tells you not to be trans. But the system lies. The system makes people trans even while it blames them for being trans. The system argues on a loop and makes people cross the desert over and over again.

If you are upset about being trans, there are options. The system can take away your trans autonomy, invent a mental disorder, diagnose you, and tell you it is pleased by your suffering because your trans distress is a prerequisite for it to give you anything that could enable your trans joy. We can see if that long process helps. If it does not, the system can delete the mental disorder from the books as if it had never been written. We can see if we stand at the beginning again.

I know I don't need to be sarcastic, but neither do you need to be upset about being trans.

This is life on the margin. We are suffering and joyful and we try things that don't work and we try again.

For good measure: If you have ever called anyone else trans, you too were trans before that word left your lips.

So it is fair that you are made trans. The margin you observe others walking is the same margin you walk.

Let it happen.

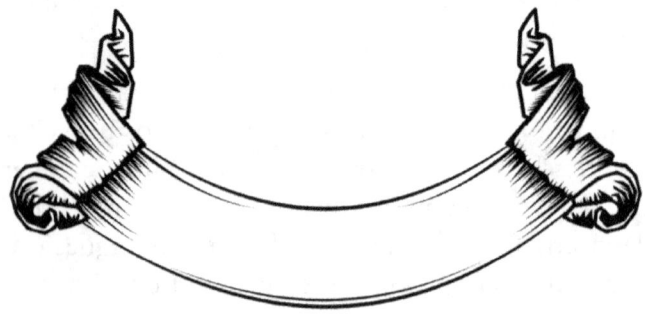

When I am not expecting it, an invitation comes. It arrives from space. Not from the stars; not that far. Only from a satellite. Written words appear on the screen in my pocket. The text message is not spiritual but worldly. I am not the seeker but the recruited.

They ask me to explain myself while they stand on one foot. My end of the conversation sounds like this:

—*Sure, I worked in technology.*

—*Created data, tested software, designed the interface.*

—*Yes, in the new methodology.*

—*Is there a language requirement? ... Oh, I see.*

We end the conversation. The talent recruiter is looking for someone who speaks Spanish. I expect it'll be hard for me to work in Bogotá since I don't speak Spanish.

Then it occurs to me: We'd had that whole conversation in Spanish.

I call them back. One, two, three, four times we have the interview. The recruiter texts me to inform me that the hiring manager "está pensando en algo para proponerte." The interface has no italics. I just have to know what the words mean. *The boss is planning to make me an offer.*

The invitation didn't come as a result of my cultivation of spiritual virtues. I've done nothing specifically to deserve this.

It's just that, as you see above, I've started to write English in italics. So it is time.

The invitation may have come because of the way people perceive my gender, race, nationality, age, physical ability, and weight. I may surprise them. I'm a white man; I'm also trans and Jewish. I have a U.S. passport and a Colombian visa I must renew every three years. Yes, I'm aging every day, I weigh something, I'm telling myself I can still jog to the office; no, I'm not trying to control myself. I am flowering.

The invitation very definitely has to do with my language. The air I breathed in Boston is an asset in Bogotá. Yes, I need to speak Spanish too, but they're not hiring me for my Spanish. They want me to write English the way I learned to write it in Boston. They want me to ask Boston to dance.

I hope they are not disappointed that I only know how to write books that make people trans.

They don't give me the job because the company decides it has no money to hire me after all. At least, that's what they said. Maybe they looked me up, saw the trans, and were afraid I'd make them trans.

I'm disappointed I don't have their money, but I'm happy I don't have to go to the office.

I've been in denial about the severity of my foot injuries so it would have been hard to walk to the office anyway.

I am not in a rush.

Eventually, someone else comes with another invitation. This second invitation is the one that sticks.

There is no office to go to; I work from home. This changes the meaning of work, or at least how I perceive this work, and how my body-mind does the work.

my husband is writing a novel exploring the Colombian myth of Patasola, "One Paw." In some versions of the myth, her husband hacked off one of her legs and tossed it on a bonfire. In others, God punished her for sexual sin by sewing her legs together. In any case, she hops along in the woods, one-legged, and if you hear her, you should run.

He's been writing the novel for several years. Patasola does not walk at the same speed that others do. Be patient. She's there, and she will come out.

i realize work has meant something to me and I've assumed it means the same to everyone else, but it does not.

Most people work for money they need. Some are also motivated to work for extra money they want. Some seek status; they expect their work will make them important. Some develop their skills. Or they build community with their coworkers, clients, and wider network. They feel they're "supposed" to work, and that finding a job will help them find a lover or a mate, and that holding a merely acceptable job will someday allow them to advance to a better job.

Some of these motivations have been mine at various times. But for me, there's something much bigger, something so omnipresent it has been invisible to me.

I believed — in an Enlightenment philosophy kind of way, in a liberal way — that everyone has rights that are always fragile or threatened. To address this, an academic strategy is to read and write philosophy. A long-term practical strategy is to enact yourself as a human being in society so that when the persecutors come for you, you can gather your neighbors, point to your own human life, and argue that you should be allowed to continue to live. The self-humanizing strategy sounds at first blush as though it will work, but it may be no more effective than philosophy.

I think that everyone who is in some way marginalized, especially those who put effort into assimilating or "passing," will immediately know what I mean. Particularly those of us who have ever had to put effort into causing or requesting others to perceive us as "a man" or "a woman" and who have ever sought to avoid being primarily marked as trans or queer before we are seen simply in our gender.

I passed for cis in an office full of hundreds of cis people, not bringing up the fact that I was a post-transition transsexual. I guess I was trying to humanize myself in their eyes. This was my social insurance in case the Nazis ever came for me or for other trans people. If the moment came, so I believed, I could out myself, and as long as I was already medium-liked, my visibility and my plea would save us all. That was part of my fantasy about who we all were at the office. I was playing Queen Esther in boy drag, year-round. Sorry for the shpiel.

Here's a big unanswered question, though: When should you do the big reveal? Should you anticipate your loss of rights and come out strategically at an early stage of fascism? If so, when? If you imagine yourself accruing humanity points by staying in the closet, you'll want to stay in there as long as possible so you emerge fully funded with pocketfuls of humanity points, but these points have expiration dates, which is to say that you shouldn't wait until all the cis people have decided they don't believe trans people should exist because then it'll be too late to educate them otherwise. Nazi tanks rolling in can't be your dramatic cue to speak up; not only would it be too late, but, just as drowning doesn't look like yelling and waving, radicalization doesn't look like swastikas. Everyone looks like a person.

I worked eleven years for this company without coming out as trans. I'd spent more than half my post-transition era in that office. I had to leave for my own reasons. I never had the chance to unmask and give them the teaching moment about my own humanity and the humanity of all trans people. Anyway, I never knew how to explain it, and they were never going to listen. With respect to that goal, those eleven years were wasted years.

Meanwhile, fascism has rolled in. I didn't even manage to tell a cis person I was trans. I wasn't using the short-form word *trans*, hence I couldn't see the value in *cis*, and since I didn't have basic words, I wasn't writing Enlightenment-style philosophy.

I'm starting over.

"This book is my Shield," said A.V. Marraccini of her own work of criticism, *We The Parasites*. She's invoking the Shield of Achilles: a detailed work of art, a microcosm of the known world, a representation of the epic conflict.

The Shield, it seems, enables transformation.

> I will consume all that is before me, but I will burn instead of it... I will grow an extra set of legs, but stand in the back of the crowd and be amenable during the cocktail hour...

> I will unfurl my wet wings into the expectant space of the air, far from the nation of my birth, and fly...[107]

Six years after I resigned, I wrote to one of the vice presidents to ask if we could speak on the phone.

I knew which of our mutual colleagues (someone who still worked at the company) maintained a secret social media account entirely dedicated to racist, anti-immigrant, transphobic, homophobic memes and to the valorization of the weapons used in mass shootings. I was ready to tell the vice president what I knew. I wanted to ask permission to tell her about this. I felt morally injured by keeping it a secret. If a secretly hateful person, especially one who is armed, is inside the company, the situation may someday affect the vice president personally and the people with whom she works. This affects us all as human beings. A situation like this influences our decisions of which countries we'll live in.

Having asked for a phone call, I began the conversation by asking for permission to go into details about my reason for the call. I told the vice president that I was anxious about something and that I wanted to tell her exactly what it was.

She spent fifteen minutes telling me to speak to a therapist or go outside and touch grass.

I struggled to find the right words to argue with her suggestion about the therapist. There's nothing wrong with speaking to a therapist, and I was resolved not to imply that there is. However, whether I have a psychotherapist was irrelevant to my message and furthermore wasn't her business. The information I wanted to provide to the vice president was of actionable value to her alone.

"I want to talk *to you*," I said.

She seemed to think I was stubbornly demanding that she be my therapist.

Regarding her suggestion of going out to get fresh air, I shared with her that her casual recommendation didn't really fit my needs because I had arthritis. I imagined I was humoring her small-talk by adding relevant detail building on what she'd said and humanizing myself by sharing this vulnerable detail about my arthritis.

Finally she understood: I wanted to give her information. She said she'd talk to some people about it.

A week passed. She texted back, informing me that the company already monitors employees' social media accounts. (I knew this. I'd wanted to tell her they hadn't caught the big one.)

White people should use our power to talk to other white people about stopping racism. We should try, and we should be aware that it won't always work. Sure, Queen Esther was successful as a supplicant to the King, but Queen Esther in boy drag may have had a different outcome.

White trans people are white. White trans people are trans.

Even if other white people do not consciously know we're trans, something about our actual transness may send our calls to their voicemail. We may be prepared to disclose that we're trans if they would be listening, but they are not listening because we're trans. It is hard to talk to the cis-tem from a place of transness. Also Jewishness.

"I hope your feet continue to feel better," the vice president wrote me, "so that you can enjoy that Colombian weather!"

I'd run in so many circles around Boston in the snow, I'd unintentionally lost a huge amount of weight and given myself acid reflux and arthritis.

What she'd said on the phone had been a little more specific, more like: *Get more exercise so you're less insane.*

She must not know how my insanity works.

Enjoy the weather was the limited euphemism she put in writing. This is corporate-speak for saying the company doesn't have time to care whether someone is trying to kill them and their employees if the only way for them to get that information would be to acknowledge that I exist and that I care about them.

They're telling me: *Over our own dead bodies will we listen to you, ever, about anything.*

In other words, I was invited to take a hike.

Not with the vice presidents on the golf course. With myself. Through the Andes Mountains, three thousand miles away, into eternity. It would be convenient for them if I did not have arthritis because then I could walk farther away.

When people tell us they will never listen to us, one thing we can do is break up with them.

Tressie McMillan Cottom says:

> you will absolutely positively have to break up with actual white people. ... It...isn't my ministry to write a secular Pentateuch for the people who have broken up with the white people who tether them to whiteness but I do believe there is one. I believe there is not only a way to live after the break-up but that you do not start living until you break-up.[108]

In that office, I showed up as a man, and never could I and never will I be visible to them as trans.

I provide these details, literally and directly, so you can understand what I mean by trauma that is trans.

In the second edition of this book, I said the book will make you trans. I thought that might be a new trick. A year later, Cameron Awkward-Rich published *The Terrible We* in which he said: "It is a commonplace within trans worlds that reading in a trans way might, in fact, make you trans."[109]

Oh. Well, let my trick be commonplace; I welcome it; commonplace at last, I feel seen.

First Kings 19:11-13:

> "Come out," God called, "and stand on the mountain before God." God passed by. There was a great and mighty wind, splitting mountains and shattering rocks by God's power; but God was not in the wind. After the wind—an earthquake; but God was not in the earthquake. After the earthquake—fire;

but God was not in the fire. And after the fire—a soft murmuring sound. When Elijah heard it, he wrapped his mantle around his face and went out and stood at the entrance of the cave. Then a voice addressed him: "Why are you here, Elijah?"[110]

I listen to the still, small voice and think about ways I've been complicit. Around age 15, when I could have chosen the name Elijah because I am a Jew, I chose the name Tucker simply because it appealed to me. I didn't have many deep thoughts about why it appealed to me. Even though no one by this name had a talk show yet, I could have told you that the name didn't reflect my ethnicity. I have leaned into whiteness from the beginning of my trans without seeing that I was doing so, without knowing why, but not without consequences.

Rabbi Zusya of Hanipol, according to Martin Buber, used to say: "If they ask me in the next world, 'Why were you not Moses?' I will know the answer. But if they ask me, 'Why were you not Zusya?' I will have nothing to say."[111]

Each of us has to be ourselves.

And each of us has to change.

One year after I failed to communicate anything to the vice president, seven years after I left Boston, nine years after the Grave Incident, I observed for the ten-thousandth time that I was having a hard time letting go.

I thought: *Moses wouldn't have a hard time letting go. He never did. When the boys hurt him, he declared "the boys are dead," and that was that.*

How can I be more like Moses?

No, wait — how can I be more like me?

What's a rude magic phrase I can speak to interrupt myself from caring about the vice presidents who never cared about me?

Better nine years late than never, I have it: *The goys are dead.*

I do not believe in God, but I know something about faith. It is about being transformed without being consumed. It is a skill. Caterpillars, chrysalides, butterflies have it.

The chrysalis may taste bad to predators. That is the point. The caterpillar does not want a motivational speech about its career. Do not ask it where it wants to be in five years. The caterpillar does not want unsolicited advice about how it can look sharper at work. It doesn't care if it's fat; it isn't walking anywhere right now and isn't worried about its hip joint. If it's starting to lose weight, it isn't intentional. The caterpillar does not need self-help books or coaching to do what it is doing, though it can receive the gift of a lantern moon as it goes eyes-open into the nighttime journey it will be taking anyway. Something outside its control has started to happen. The caterpillar's immune system says NOPE and its imaginal discs say YUP. Part of it isn't ready and part of it is. *Ready or not.* It's unstable and that's what causes its tectonic shift within.

Do not, in an accusatory tone or sarcastic sneer or in any way that disinvites the possibility of an honest answer, ask if it is *all right.* The caterpillar is preparing to weave a cocoon. It is not all right. It is about to leave its old self behind forever. Its house is burning, and the situation is not "fine." Even its internal organs will melt and reform.

You absolutely cannot touch it at this time. You will give it shpilkes in the kishkes, anxious ants in the guts. If you put the smallest pinprick in the cocoon, the insect will emerge horribly deformed, if it survives at all: no hip, all hip. So you leave it alone for a long time. You let it talk to God.

"You're not doing your work," says God.

"I know. I'm sorry," says the khilazon.

"You don't need to be so fragile," says God.

"But my transformation is about me," says the khilazon.

"I'm calling you out," says God.

"I'm so ashamed," says the khilazon.

"No, I mean I'm calling you out," says God. *"I want you out of the cocoon. Now."*

What is the voice? If it's God, how does God fit inside the cocoon that's already full of butterfly? If it's the butterfly's imagination, how is the insect capable of generating the idea that it must break the silk walls that have been holding it together to once again hatch a more advanced version of itself?

It will finally poke a hole in its orthopedic harness and crawl out. It lets the harness fall. The harness is ex. The creature has six proper butterfly hips and two wings. It is correctly formed, even though you don't recognize it then. It doesn't recognize the world because it has new eyes, new feelers, a new tongue, and it lifts itself high on the wind. Its body is trans, inside and out. It is expatriated, flying thousands of miles to mate. It says a great big Mourner's Kaddish for itself: *Blessed and praised, glorified and exalted, extolled and honored, adored and lauded, abundant peace from heaven, harmony on high – according to the way the world will be.*

None of this is OK. But this is life.

There are real experiences of trans trauma and there are realities we call trans joy.

"*Be careful out there,*" says God.

"*I always have been,*" says the khilazon, fluttering away.

"*Glass beads shatter,*" says God.

"*I can't hear you,*" the khilazon shouts.

"*Nine tears of the night,*" God yells after it.

Women are not fine when they are giving birth. Men are not fine when they are shooting at each other. People who fall through the floorboards of that binary are not fine when we are seeing a specter no one else sees. It is painful and stressful. We are seeing blood that isn't the color of blood because it belongs to an insect. We are seeing a spider's tiny florid handiwork. We are seeing a natural logarithm. It looks like the flight path of a butterfly with wet wings. We are seeing a Fibonacci sequence. It looks like the center of a sunflower. It feels like a hip joint that has yet to click into some unconsciously fantasized golden ratio. There are clues. We have to find our own balance. No one tells us where to run. No one tells us when to push.

The butterfly will dream itself into being.

"Even as your chest / fills with a strange new air, you will not ask / what this means," Rickey Laurentiis writes in their poem "You Are Not Christ."

"Like prey caught in the wolf's teeth, / but you are not the lamb. You are what's in the lamb / that keeps it kicking. Let it."[112]

The sacred blue dye may never been in the caterpillar, or in the cocoon, or in anything, but now the butterfly sees it: *The sky. The sky.* Blue from its edges, its edges rooted to nowhere and everywhere, blue seeping into the world, uncontrollable, unstoppable. *Holy, holy.* The butterfly didn't need to worry about emerging on time. The schedule is perfectly aligned. Messiah has just now arrived and has brought the *tekhelet*.

The butterfly will learn to sip nectar. It will be less hungry. Its same old thoughts will come to it in another language.

What is different is not an opposite. Lo diferente no es lo contrario.

It will be part of the sun. It is forming itself to seek warmth and light. It will have photoreceptors in its wings and in its penis.

Aren't you glad you asked what kind of penis it has. Qué contento debes estar de haber preguntado por su pene.

It will hear its name pronounced differently. It may choose not to come when it is called. It will finally meditate. Its flight will be the meditation. It will go.

Sic transit gloria mundi. The glory of the world is trans.

That is what the caterpillar will become. Yet when the caterpillar closes its cocoon, it does not know for certain if it will ever see light again. It acts on an inner drive. It listens to the secret color of its blood. It grows little wings tilted in italics. It sheds what held it back.

It doesn't know what it's doing and it won't explain itself to you. It needs to make itself taste bad to others for a while. It will use its own stored energy.

As the wings dry, they'll unitalicize. The butterfly will take flight in its own language.

Wait. Watch. Stop criticizing.

When it unfolds, it will be totally fire.

a־brought the author

Firewalking, age 38, July 21, 2018.
Alexandria Mauck Photography

TUCKER LIEBERMAN is the author of *Ten Past Noon: Focus and Fate at Forty* (2020), a biography of a New York writer who died by suicide. His bilingual poetry collection inspired by the Epic of Gilgamesh, *Enkidu is Dead and Not Dead / Enkidu está muerto y no lo está*, was a finalist for the Grayson Books poetry prize (2020).

Originally from Boston, Massachusetts, he lives with the science fiction writer Arturo Serrano in Bogotá, Colombia.

He is also the author of *Painting Dragons: What Storytellers Need to Know About Writing Eunuch Villains* (2018).

He had a sex change when the Internet was dial-up. He then became an early adopter of same-sex marriage and shortly afterward of same-sex divorce. He does many things inexpertly. He spent a summer on a canoe expedition in Northern Ontario and another summer shadowing U.S. Army ROTC cadets at Fort Knox. He worked for a decade in technology for an investment company, received the FINRA Series 7 license, and trained as a life coach at the Easton Mountain retreat center for gay men. He was born with a deformed hip and has run a half-marathon at his own speed. He has walked on fire.

WWW.TUCKERLIEBERMAN.COM

sight-ashes

---

[1] Rachel Vorona Cote. *Too Much: How Victorian Constraints Still Bind Women Today.* New York: Grand Central Publishing, 2020.

[2] Lance Olsen. "Debris as debris, or cutting room floor as a state of mind." Dzanc Books. April 3, 2017. https://www.dzancbooks.org/blog/2017/4/3/countdownto pub-debris-as-debris-or-cutting-room-floor-as-a-state-of-mind

[3] Arthur W. Frank. *The Wounded Storyteller: Body, Illness, and Ethics.* (Originally published 1995.) Second edition. Chicago and London: The University of Chicago Press, 2013. pp. 97, 103, 99, 69.

[4] Tucker Lieberman. "What Can We Make of the Death of Aaron's Sons?," JewishBoston, March 7, 2019.

Tucker Lieberman. "The Suicide of Nadav and Abihu," *Shalom Magazine.* Passover/Spring 2019.

[5] David Abram. *The Spell of the Sensuous: Perception and Language in a More-Than-Human World.* (Originally 1996.) Vintage, 2012.

[6] KC Green. "On Fire." *Gunshow.* 2013. http://gunshowcomic.com/648

[7] The commentary of Rabbi Shlomo Yitzchaki (Rashi) has informed Jewish tradition for nearly a thousand years and can be found online at Sefaria: https://www.sefaria.org/Rashi_on_Leviticus.10.6?lang=bi

[8] Elyn R. Saks. *The Center Cannot Hold: My Journey Through Madness.* New York: Hyperion, 2007. pp. 12-13.

[9] Matthew Salesses. "Holding It Together, Falling Apart: On Living Through Grief, Both Collective and Personal." *LitHub*. Sept. 8, 2020. https://lithub.com/matthew-salesses-holding-it-together-falling-apart/

[10] Lauren Berlant. *Cruel Optimism*. Durham and London: Duke University Press, 2011. p. 6.

[11] Hartley Lachter. "Silkworms of Exile: Jewish History and Collective Memory in the Kabbalistic Works of Meir ibn Gabbai." Shofar, Vol. 40, No. 3., 2022, pp. 1-37. p. 4. https://doi.org/10.1353/sho.2022.0028 Accessed April 27, 2023.

[12] Ellen Bass. "Change." http://divinesparks.blogspot.com/2010/11/change-ellen-bass.html Accessed October 16, 2020.

[13] Juana de Ibarbourou. "Mujer" (1922). Reprinted in *Twentieth-Century Latin American Poetry: A Bilingual Anthology*. ed. Stephen Tapscott. Austin, Texas: University of Texas Press, 1996. p. 127. The translation I've provided here is my own. Tapscott's anthology contains a different English translation by Sophie Cabot Black.

[14] Rita Dove's poem "History" was originally published in the journal *Caprice*. It was subsequently included in her book *Mother Love* (1995). It was also reprinted in *Mississippi Review*.

[15] Zechariah 3:2.

[16] Benjamin Zander. "Radiate Possibility and Make Fascinating Mistakes." Pop Tech Conference. 2008. https://www.theatrefolk.com/blog/radiate-possibility-and-make-fascinating-mistakes/ (Video location: 10:40-55)

[17] Peter Chadwick. "Sanity to supersanity to insanity: a personal journey." Printed in *Psychosis and Spirituality: Exploring the New Frontier*. ed. Isabel Clarke. London and

Philadelphia: Whurr, 2001. p. 78.

I was unable to locate Peter Chadwick and am unsure what pronouns he might be using today. The last available pronouns I found for him were masculine.

[18] Natalie Eilbert. "Imaginal Discs." *Mississippi Review.* Winter 2019, Volume 46, Number 3.

[19] Martin Buber. *Hasidic Tales.* In the preface to *Early Masters.* (Translated by Olga Marx.) New York: Schocken, 1947. Quoted in "Avodah: The Story of the High Priest," by Rabbi Dov Peretz Elkins, in *Yom Kippur Readings: Inspiration, Information and Contemplation.* ed. Dov Peretz Elkins. Woodstock, Vt.: Jewish Lights, 2005. p. 229.

[20] Babylonian Talmud. Shabbat 31a.

[21] Tucker Lieberman. "The Trail of His Flames." *It Came From the Closet: Queer Reflections on Horror.* ed. Joe Vallese. New York: Feminist Press, 2022. p. 177.

[22] Kiese Laymon. *Heavy: An American Memoir.* Scribner, 2018. The sentence he cites is from James Baldwin's essay "Faulkner and Desegregation" printed in *Nobody Knows My Name.*

[23] Tucker Lieberman, "The Trail of His Flames," p. 172.

[24] Arthur W. Frank, op. cit., p. 38.

[25] Dale Stromberg. *Mæj.* Munich: tRaum Books, 2024.

[26] Hil Malatino. *Trans Care.* Minneapolis and London: University of Minnesota Press, 2020.

[27] Malatino, op. cit.

[28] Elizabeth Deanna Morris Lakes. "Ashley Doesn't Know." *Ashley Sugarnotch & The Wolf.* Baltimore: Mason Jar Press, 2020. p. 31.

[29] Devin Kelly. "Out There: On Not Finishing." *Longreads*. September 2020. https://longreads.com/2020/09/08/out-there-on-not-finishing/

[30] Abram J. Lewis. "'I Am 64 and Paul McCartney Doesn't Care': The Haunting of the Transgender Archive and the Challenges of Queer History." *Radical History Review*, no. 120 (2014): 13–34. p. 27. doi 10.1215/01636545-2703697 https://transreads.org/wp-content/uploads/2022/01/2022-01-07_61d7881623504_Iam64.pdf

[31] Cameron Awkward-Rich. *The Terrible We: Thinking With Trans Maladjustment*. Durham and London: Duke University Press, 2022. p. 58.

[32] Del Samatar and Sofia Samatar. *Monster Portraits*. Brookline, Mass.: Rose Metal Press, 2018.

[33] Awkward-Rich, op. cit., pp. 8, 11.

[34] Elisa Gabbert. "The Great Mortality," in *The Unreality of Memory, and Other Essays*. New York: Farrar, Straus and Giroux, 2020.

[35] Naomi Klein. *On Fire: The (Burning) Case for a Green New Deal*. New York: Simon & Schuster, 2019.

[36] Lauren Berlant, op. cit., p. 122.

[37] Sam Sax. *Yr Dead*. San Francisco: McSweeney's, 2024. p. 254.

[38] Peter Chadwick, op. cit., pp. 75, 85.

[39] "It would, of course, be hubristic to attempt a definitive etiology of the apparent madness that marked many of these lives, and yet this madness has imposed itself on me with such intensity that it has become nearly inconceivable as anything other than systemic, as somehow symptomatic of the destructive forces in which these infelicitous subjects were caught." Abram J. Lewis, op. cit., p. 24.

[40] Quoted by Leonard Fein. *Where Are We?: The Inner Life of America's Jews.* New York: Harper and Row, 1988. p. 133.

[41] Erik Davis. *High Weirdness: Drugs, Esoterica, and Visionary Experience in the Seventies.* London: Strange Attractor Press, 2019. He says: "Many have pointed out that the term *altered* implies that these states are distortions of a foundational baseline consciousness that anchors all the other transformations, rather than indicating modes of consciousness with their own autonomy and integral character. Similarly, the term *states* is arguably too static and discrete to cover experiential zones that are more often characterized by boundary dissolution and montage, drift and resonance." For an example of this interpretation of the term *altered*, he refers to Charles Tart's 1971 introduction to the second edition of *Altered States of Consciousness.*

[42] Zenju Earthlyn Manuel. *Opening to Darkness: Eight Gateways for Being with the Absence of Light in Unsettling Times.* Boulder, Colo.: Sounds True, 2023. She references Andrew Harvey, *Experience Renewal Through the Global Dark Night: Finding Your Purpose and Strength by Embracing the Mystical Meaning Behind the Crisis,* podcast, produced by the Shift Network, September 26, 2020.

[43] Anthony Johnson, speaking in Episode 68 of Gen R: "Two-Spirit, Cree Physician Revolutionizes Trans Care." AJ+. October 18, 2020.

https://www.facebook.com/ajplusenglish/posts/1963767930431371

[44] Arthur W. Frank, op. cit. p. 9.

[45] Winifred Gallagher. *Rapt: Attention and the Focused Life.* New York: Penguin, 2009. p. 88.

[46] Jim Wallis. *The Soul of Politics: Beyond 'Religious Right' and 'Secular Left'.* New York: Harvest, 1995. p. 169.

[47] Malatino, op. cit.

[48] Awkward-Rich, op. cit., p. 4.

[49] James Baldwin. "Faulkner and Desegregation." Originally published in *Partisan Review* (Fall 1956) and reprinted in his essay collection *Nobody Knows My Name* (Dial Press, 1961).

[50] Mihaly Csikszentmihalyi. *Flow: The Psychology of Optimal Experience*. Harper Perennial Modern Classics, 1990. pp. 41-42.

[51] Esmé Weijun Wang. *The Collected Schizophrenias*. Minneapolis: Graywolf Press, 2019.

[52] Abram J. Lewis. op. cit., p. 24. Quoting Avery Gordon, *Ghostly Matters: Haunting and the Sociological Imagination* (Minneapolis: University of Minnesota Press, 2008), pp. xvi, 25.

[53] *Kilkul* means "spiritual damage," and it is the opposite of *tikkun*, which means "spiritual rectification," according to Gabriella Samuel in *The Kabbalah Handbook: A Concise Encyclopedia of Terms and Concepts in Jewish Mysticism*. TarcherPerigee, 2007.

"...one person's *tikkun* may be another's *kilkul* (rupture or breakdown)." Jeremy Benstein. *The Way Into Judaism and the Environment*. Woodstock, Vt.: Jewish Lights Publishing, 2006. p. 111.

[54] "Schizophrenics are victims of the Russian word гибель (*gibel*), which is synonymous with 'doom' and 'catastrophe' — not necessarily death nor suicide, but a ruinous cessation of existence; we deteriorate in a way that is painful for others...other human catastrophes can bear the weight of human narrative — war, kidnapping, death — but schizophrenia's built-in chaos resists sense," writes Esmé Weijun Wang. A term like *gibel* can also "address the suffering of those who are adjacent to the one who is suffering in the first place." Esmé Weijun Wang. *The Collected Schizophrenias*. Minneapolis: Graywolf Press, 2019.

[55] La Marr Jurelle Bruce. "Mad Is a Place; or, the Slave Ship Tows the Ship of Fools." *American Quarterly*, Volume 69, Number 2, June 2017, pp. 303–308. Johns Hopkins University Press. DOI: https://doi.org/10.1353/aq.2017.0024 p. 307.

[56] Elaine Wang. "A Caterpillar Chewing a Weed Leaf Wonders if He'll Ever Become a Butterfly." *Dust Poetry*. September 2020. https://www.dustpoetry.co.uk/post/a-caterpillar-chewing-a-weed-leaf-wonders-if-he-ll-ever-become-a-butterfly-by-elaine-wang

[57] Gregory Nazianzen. Oration XXXVII: "On the Words of the Gospel, 'When Jesus Had Finished These Sayings,' Etc.— S. Matt. 19:1." Sections XVI and XVII.

[58] Sam Sax, op. cit. p. 50.

[59] Patrick Harpur. *The Philosopher's Secret Fire: A History of the Imagination* (2002). Chicago: Ivan R. Dee, 2003. p. 264.

[60] Sam Sax, op. cit. p. 188.

[61] Markham Heid. "You Asked: Is Watching Scary Movies Good For You?" *Time*. October 25, 2017. http://time.com/4995896/scary-movies-burn-calories/

[62] Angel Olsen. "White Fire." In the 2014 album *Burn Your Fire for No Witness*. Quoted by Jack Brendan Miller as the epigraph to GLORY/TREE/GHOST, Bone & Ink, 2020.

[63] Steven Church. *One With the Tiger: Sublime and Violent Encounters Between Humans and Animals*. Berkeley, Calif.: Soft Skull Press, 2016. p. 18.

[64] Federico García Lorca. "Juego y teoría del duende," a lecture given to la Sociedad de Amigos del Arte in Buenos Aires, October 20, 1933. https://www.taurologia.com/imagenes/fotosdeldia/1909_federico_garcia_lorca__juego_y_teoria_del_duende__.pdf

⁶⁵ Lance Olsen. "Debris as debris, or cutting room floor as a state of mind." Dzanc Books. April 3, 2017. https://www.dzancbooks.org/blog/2017/4/3/countdownto pub-debris-as-debris-or-cutting-room-floor-as-a-state-of-mind

⁶⁶ Terry Eagleton. *The Ideology of the Aesthetic*. Oxford: Blackwell, 1990, pp.163-4. Quoted by Elisa Gabbert, "Big and Slow," in *The Unreality of Memory, and Other Essays*. New York: Farrar, Straus and Giroux, 2020.

⁶⁷ Lewis Raven Wallace. *The View From Somewhere: Undoing the Myth of Journalistic Objectivity*. Chicago and London: The University of Chicago Press, 2019. Chapter 10.

⁶⁸ Arthur W. Frank, op. cit. "Preface, 2013."

⁶⁹ Frank, op. cit. p. 154.

⁷⁰ "Debbie Friedman, Singer of Jewish Music, Dies at 59." Margalit Fox. New York Times. January 11, 2011. http://www.nytimes.com/2011/01/11/arts/music/11friedman.html

⁷¹ Jennifer Finney Boylan. *She's Not There: A Life in Two Genders*. New York: Broadway Books, 2003. p. 248.

⁷² Rabbi Danya Ruttenberg. Twitter. March 12, 2020. https://twitter.com/TheRaDR/status/1238240758739730434 Accessed December 30, 2020.

⁷³ Esther J. Hamori. *God's Monsters: Vengeful Spirits, Deadly Angels, Hybrid Creatures, and Divine Hitmen of the Bible*. Minneapolis: Broadleaf Books, 2023. Chapter 6: Manipulative and Mind-Altering Spirits.

⁷⁴ JK Anowe. "Etc." Printed in *Memento: An Anthology of Contemporary Nigerian Poetry*. Edited by Adedayo Agarau. Thetford Center, Vt.: *Animal Heart Press*, 2020. p. 16.

⁷⁵ Blackiston DJ, Silva Casey E, Weiss MR (2008) "Retention of Memory through Metamorphosis: Can a Moth Remember What It Learned As a Caterpillar?" *PLoS*

ONE 3(3): e1736. https://doi.org/10.1371/journal.pone.0001736

[76] Ellen Bass, "Indigo." *The New Yorker*, 2017. https://poets.org/poem/indigo

[77] Elaine Wang. "A Caterpillar Chewing a Weed Leaf Wonders if He'll Ever Become a Butterfly." *Dust Poetry*. September 2020. https://www.dustpoetry.co.uk/post/a-caterpillar-chewing-a-weed-leaf-wonders-if-he-ll-ever-become-a-butterfly-by-elaine-wang

[78] Minna Salami. *Sensuous Knowledge: A Black Feminist Approach For Everyone*. Amistad, 2020. Chapter 6: Of Womanhood. The woman in the story is the goddess Asi of the Foya Kamara. Salami attributes this telling of the story to Esther Sietmann Warner Dendel.

[79] Giorgio Agamben. *The Fire and the Tale*. Originally *Il fuoco e il racconto*, 2014. Translated by Lorenzo Chiesa. Stanford, California: Stanford University Press, 2017. Agamben tells this parable in the opening chapter, "The Fire and the Tale." He cites it to Gershom Scholem, who says he learned it from Yosef Agnon.

[80] Rainer Maria Rilke. "Das Einhorn." Winter 1905/06. http://rainer-maria-rilke.de/080029daseinhorn.html The English is my own translation.

[81] Alok Vaid-Menon. *Beyond the Gender Binary*. New York: Penguin Workshop, 2020.

[82] Devin Kelly. "Running Dysmorphic." *Longreads*. December 2019. https://longreads.com/2019/12/04/running-dysmorphic/

[83] Manuel, op. cit.

[84] Malatino, op. cit.

[85] Jessica Steinberg. "Shiri Maimon offers potent cover of

Israeli classic, 'Bashana Haba'a.'" *Times of Israel.* September 17, 2020. https://www.timesofisrael.com/shiri-maimon-offers-potent-cover-of-israeli-classic-bashana-habaa/

[86] The final line of the poem "Ashley Doesn't Know" is: "I sold the house." Elizabeth Deanna Morris Lakes. "Ashley Doesn't Know." *Ashley Sugarnotch & The Wolf.* Baltimore: Mason Jar Press, 2020. p. 31.

[87] Gershon Winkler. *Magic of the Ordinary: Recovering the Shamanic in Judaism.* Berkeley, Calif.: North Atlantic Books, 2003. pp. 24-25.

[88] Dan Barker. *Free Will Explained: How Science and Philosophy Converge to Create a Beautiful Illusion.* New York: Sterling, 2018. p. 29.

[89] Patrick Harpur, op. cit., p. 150.

[90] Audre Lorde, *The Cancer Journals,* 61. Quoted in Arthur W. Frank, op. cit.

[91] Ellen Bass, "Change," op. cit.

[92] Devin Kelly. "Out There: On Not Finishing." op. cit.

[93] Peter Chadwick, op. cit. p. 77.

[94] E. M. Cioran. *The Trouble With Being Born.* (1973) (Trans. by Richard Howard.) New York: Arcade, 2012.

[95] Leslie Streeter. *Black Widow: A Sad-Funny Journey Through Grief for People Who Normally Avoid Books with Words Like 'Journey' in the Title.* New York: Little, Brown and Company, 2020. Chapter 11.

[96] Rachel A. Rosen. *Cascade: The Sleep of Reason* (Book 1). Ottawa: BumblePuppy, 2022.

[97] Elyn R. Saks, op. cit., p. 32.

[98] "Kati Standefer on the Mysterious Leslie Ryan and the Structure of a Trauma Narrative." *Essay Daily.* March 11,

2013. https://www.essaydaily.org/2013/03/kati-standefer-on-mysterious-leslie.html

[99] This Yiddish imprecation was used in the story "The Red Dybbuk" in Barbara Krasnoff's collection *The History of Soul 2065*. Mythic Delirium, 2019.

[100] Zander Nethercutt, "The End of Authenticity: Why do all coffeeshops look alike?" *Buy Yourself* (Medium). April 25, 2018. https://medium.com/s/buy-yourself/the-end-of-authenticity-bd858bc3b413

[101] Tucker Lieberman, op. cit., p. 187.

[102] Natalie Eilbert. "Imaginal Discs." *Mississippi Review*. Winter 2019, Volume 46, Number 3.

[103] Russell Hoban. *Pilgermann*. London: Bloomsbury, 1983. Chapter 1.

[104] Rabbi Ora Weiss pointed out that "the very center of the Torah is the white space between the two words" in a 2020 paper titled "Your Doorway to Freedom."

[105] Awkward-Rich, op. cit., p. 147.

[106] Mihaly Csikszentmihalyi. *Flow: The Psychology of Optimal Experience*. Harper Perennial Modern Classics, 1990. pp. 41–42.

[107] A.V. Marraccini. *We the Parasites*. Sublunary Editions, 2023. pp. 138–139.

[108] Tressie McMillan Cottom, "Breaking Up With White Supremacy Was Always The End Game," Medium, January 24, 2021. https://tressiemcphd.medium.com/breaking-up-with-white-supremacy-was-always-the-end-game-e7101f578363

[109] Awkward-Rich, op. cit., p. 128. He points to Jay Prosser, *Second Skins: The Body Narratives of Transsexuality*, chaps. 3 and 4; Patricia Gherovici, *Please Select Your Gender: From the Invention of Hysteria to the Democratizing of Transgenderism*,

chap. 10. Henry Rubin, *Self-Made Men: Identity and Embodiment among Transsexual Men*, chap. 4. Judith Butler, "Undiagnosing Gender," in *Undoing Gender*, p. 81.

[110] Based on the translation of the JPS Tanakh: Gender-Sensitive Edition (Revised JPS, 2023).

[111] Martin Buber. Quoted by Ronald S. Miller and the editors of the New Age Journal. *As Above, So Below: Paths to Spiritual Renewal in Daily Life*. Los Angeles: Jeremy P. Tarcher, 1992. p. 28.

[112] Rickey Laurentiis. "You Are Not Christ." *The Collagist*. June 2010. http://thecollagist.com/the-collagist/you-are-not-christ.html

www.ingramcontent.com/pod-product-compliance
Lightning Source LLC
Chambersburg PA
CBHW071343080526
44587CB00017B/2948